P9-ECL-407
GERMANY Political Map
Names of cities over 1,000,000 are capitalized
National capitals are underlined
Secondary Boundaries
Railroads
Parts of Germany now under Polish and Russian Administration
Miles
Kilometers
COPYRIGHT BY RAND MCNALLY & COMPANY MADE IN U.S.A.
15° Longitude East of Greenwich 20°
ARCTIC OCEAN
Arctic Circle
ATLANTIC OCEAN
NORTH SEA
IRISH SEA
MEDITERRANEAN SEA
TYRRHENIAN SEA
IONIAN SEA
ADRIATIC SEA
BALTIC SEA
Bay of Biscay
English Channel
ICELAND
Reykjavík
THE FAEROES (Den.)
Tórshavn
SHETLAND IS. (Scot.)
Lerwick
ORKNEY IS.
HEBRIDES
IRELAND
Dublin
Cork
Cobh
Galway
NORTHERN IRELAND
Belfast
UNITED KINGDOM
BRITISH ISLES
SCOTLAND
WALES
ENGLAND
GLASGOW
Edinburgh
Aberdeen
Dundee
Carlisle
NEWCASTLE-ON-TYNE
LEEDS
Hull
MANCHESTER
LIVERPOOL
BIRMINGHAM
Leicester
LONDON
Southampton
Portsmouth
Dover
NORWAY
Oslo
Bergen
Stavanger
Kristiansand
Trondheim
Narvik
Hammerfest
SWEDEN
STOCKHOLM
Uppsala
Gävle
Sundsvall
Umea
Luleå
Gothenburg
Norrköping
Malmö
FINLAND
Helsinki
Turku
Oulu
Tornio
Vaasa
LAPLAND
Murmansk
Kirovsk
Kandalaksha
Pechenga
DENMARK
COPENHAGEN
Alborg
NETHERLANDS
AMSTERDAM
The Hague
ROTTERDAM
BELGIUM
BRUSSELS
ANTWERP
LUX.
FRANCE
PARIS
Calais
Lille
Le Havre
Rouen
Reims
Brest
Rennes
St. Nazaire
Nantes
Tours
Orléans
La Rochelle
Bordeaux
Clermont-Ferrand
Dijon
Lyons
Toulouse
Marseilles
Nice
Toulon
Strasbourg
GERMANY
BERLIN
HAMBURG
Bremen
Hanover
Lübeck
Kiel
Magdeburg
Leipzig
Dresden
DÜSSELDORF
ESSEN
COLOGNE
Bonn
FRANKFURT ON THE MAIN
STUTTGART
Nuremberg
MUNICH
SWITZERLAND
Bern
Zurich
Geneva
Lausanne
LIECHT.
AUSTRIA
VIENNA
Graz
ITALY
ROME
MILAN
TURIN
Genoa
Venice
Trieste
Bologna
Florence
Leghorn
NAPLES
Bari
Brindisi
Palermo
Messina
Catania
SICILY
CORSICA (Fr.)
Ajaccio
SARDINIA (It.)
MALTA
SPAIN
MADRID
BARCELONA
Valencia
Zaragoza
Valladolid
Bilbao
Santander
Oviedo
Gijón
Tarragona
Tortosa
BALEARIC ISLANDS
Palma
ANDORRA
PYRENEES
POLAND
WARSAW
Łódź
Cracow
Lublin
Wrocław
Poznań
Gdańsk
Szczecin
Toruń
Bialystok
EAST PRUSSIA
CZECHOSLOVAKIA
PRAGUE
Brno
Plzeň
Ostrava
Bratislava
HUNGARY
BUDAPEST
Szeged
Debrecen
Miskolc
YUGOSLAVIA
Belgrade
Zagreb
Ljubljana
Sarajevo
Split
Dubrovnik
Skoplje
ALBANIA
Tiranë
Durrës
Shkoder
GREECE
ATHENS
Thessaloníki
ROMANIA
BUCHAREST
Cluj
Oradea
Ploiești
Galați
Brăila
BULGARIA
Sofia
Plovdiv
Ruse
TURKEY
Edirne
U.S.S.R.
LENINGRAD
Kronshtadt
Vyborg
Tallinn
Tartu
Riga
Kaunas
Vilnius
Minsk
Grodno
Brest
Pinsk
Rovno
Lvov
Kaliningrad
ESTONIAN S.S.R.
LATVIAN S.S.R.
LITHUANIAN S.S.R.
BELORUSSIAN S.S.R.
UKRAINIAN S.S.R.
CARPATHIANS

LIFE WORLD LIBRARY

GERMANY

LIFE WORLD LIBRARY
LIFE NATURE LIBRARY
TIME READING PROGRAM
THE LIFE HISTORY OF THE UNITED STATES
LIFE SCIENCE LIBRARY
INTERNATIONAL BOOK SOCIETY
GREAT AGES OF MAN
TIME-LIFE LIBRARY OF ART
TIME-LIFE LIBRARY OF AMERICA
FOODS OF THE WORLD

LIFE WORLD LIBRARY

GERMANY

by Terence Prittie

and the Editors of

TIME-LIFE BOOKS

TIME-LIFE BOOKS NEW YORK

COVER: Well-dressed pedestrians hasten through the crowded downtown streets of rebuilt Düsseldorf, a major city of the industrial Ruhr.

ABOUT THE WRITER

Terence Prittie, the author of the interpretive text for this volume, has been a student of German affairs for many years. An Anglo-Irishman and a graduate of Christ Church, Oxford, he fought with the British army in World War II, was captured by the Germans and spent several years as a prisoner of war. In 1946 he returned to Germany as Berlin correspondent for the Manchester *Guardian*. Later he became the paper's chief German correspondent. He has traveled throughout the country, covering virtually every major postwar event for the *Guardian*. In 1963, he became the paper's diplomatic correspondent. A contributor to U.S. as well as British magazines, Mr. Prittie has written several books, including *Escape to Freedom*, a volume on notable wartime escapes; *Germany Divided: The Legacy of the Nazi Era*; and *Germans Against Hitler*.

Published simultaneously in Canada.
Library of Congress catalogue card number 61-16813.
School and library distribution by Silver Burdett Company, Morristown, New Jersey.

Contents

TIME-LIFE BOOKS

EDITOR
Maitland A. Edey
EXECUTIVE EDITOR
Jerry Korn
TEXT DIRECTOR Martin Mann
ART DIRECTOR Sheldon Cotler
CHIEF OF RESEARCH
Beatrice T. Dobie
PICTURE EDITOR
Robert G. Mason
Assistant Text Directors:
Harold C. Field, Ogden Tanner
Assistant Art Director: Arnold C. Holeywell
Assistant Chief of Research: Martha Turner

•

PUBLISHER
Rhett Austell
Associate Publisher: Walter C. Rohrer
Assistant Publisher: Carter Smith
General Manager: Joseph C. Hazen Jr.
Business Manager: John D. McSweeney
Production Manager: Louis Bronzo

•

Sales Director: Joan D. Manley
Promotion Director: Beatrice K. Tolleris
Managing Director, International: John A. Millington

LIFE WORLD LIBRARY

SERIES EDITOR: Oliver E. Allen
Editorial Staff for *Germany:*
Assistant Editor: Jay Brennan
Designer: Ben Schultz
Chief Researcher: Grace Brynolson
Researchers: Renée Pickèl, Ruth Galaid, Danuta Dorozynski, Helen R. Turvey, Linda Wolfe, Sandra Van Doren, Carol Isenberg

EDITORIAL PRODUCTION
Color Director: Robert L. Young
Copy Staff: Marian Gordon Goldman, Ann S. Lang, Patricia Miller, Florence Keith
Picture Department: Dolores A. Littles, Joan T. Lynch
Art Assistants: Douglas B. Graham, James D. Smith, Richard Forte, John M. Woods

The text for this book was written by Terence Prittie; the picture essays were written by Jay Brennan. Valuable help was provided by the following individuals and departments of Time Inc.: LIFE staff photographers Margaret Bourke-White, Ralph Crane, Eliot Elisofon, Dmitri Kessel, Michael Rougier, Burk Uzzle, Stan Wayman; Editorial Production, Robert W. Boyd Jr.; Editorial Reference, Peter Draz; Picture Collection, Doris O'Neil; Photographic Laboratory, George Karas; TIME-LIFE News Service, Richard M. Clurman.

Introduction

While we in the United States have attained the political maturity to accept our responsibilities in the world of today, we find it difficult to visualize the cold war. To the German, the cold war is a grim reality, with the boundary line between the free and communistic worlds running through the heartland of his country, patrolled on both sides by heavily armed forces. His historic capital is isolated as well as divided and subject to the constant threat of strangulation.

Any major development in the cold war seems certain to involve Berlin and Germany. Thus, for those with a sense of history, it is important to know the conditions which exist in Germany today and something of what brought them about. LIFE has provided this opportunity by including a volume on Germany in its World Library. It is fortunate to have this volume written by Terence Prittie, an astute observer who reports with accuracy in easy-to-read language.

The book is basically a report on present-day Germany, although it successfully brings in enough of the past to explain in large measure the apparent contradictions in the character of the German people. We are reminded of the almost hysterical obsession of Germany's former rulers that they would be encircled by a combination of eastern and western European nations. Today, Germany is no longer in fear of encirclement, with its territory and its people divided by an imaginary iron curtain which also marks the eastern boundary of Europe's free nations.

The importance of this boundary line to the free world leads us to ask what kind of ally we have in the Federal Republic of Germany. Outwardly, it is obviously the kind of government which we wanted to see established. It has given West Germany a thriving economy and a democratic regime which derives its authority from the people in free elections. It is a government which has chosen to become fully associated with the West and to support a closer working relationship among the countries of western Europe. We ask ourselves if this is a policy of expediency or if it represents a real determination by the people of West Germany to associate themselves with the great democracies.

Certainly, the Germans of today are neither as arrogant nor as militant as in the past. But in the pursuit of the good living, are they merely complacent, placing their political future in the hands of the professional politicians? Fortunately, there are indications that the young people of West Germany have learned to think for themselves and to show an increasing interest in their government and its acceptance of a common destiny for the free nations of Europe.

No one can answer the many questions which Mr. Prittie poses so skillfully as to the future of Germany. Personally, I believe the vast majority of the German people have chosen freedom both at home and in the world and have accepted fully the responsibilities which this choice entails. If so, their choice may be a deciding factor in the outcome of the cold war. It makes each day's report from Germany of concern to us and to our future. For the many people who have the feel for history in the making, but not the time to be its students, this book provides the background information which will make possible a more intelligent understanding of the new Germany and its role in world events.

LUCIUS D. CLAY

General, U.S. Army (ret.)
former Military Governor, U.S. Zone of Germany

In the bright afternoon sun, factory workers and office personnel from the Volkswagen plant in Wolfsburg make their way homeward

across the broad mall which leads to the company's parking lot.

1

A People of Discipline and Energy

THE dominating mood of present-day Germany is one of urgency. Life fairly hums. In Düsseldorf, a characteristic German industrial community on the Rhine River, many of the citizenry are up and about by six in the morning. The city's streets are already alive with traffic at that time, for the average German goes early to work, and no one hoping to interview a business executive should be surprised if he is told, "Come at a quarter to eight." The German on his way to his job is always in a hurry, and the formalities to which he has clung—the punctilious hat-raising to friends, the bob and bow, the standard words of greeting—are executed at the quickstep.

The pedestrians are as instinctively disciplined as Germans have been for generations. They cluster dutifully at pedestrian crossings; and warning voices—even officious ones—are always raised at the incipient jaywalker. Germans are nervous crossers of main thoroughfares, which indeed are more dangerous than those of many other European countries, and most of them suffer from a chronic sense of social and economic inferiority to the motorist.

Like any other German city, Düsseldorf has plenty of policemen on duty at complex street intersections. They are a conventional part of the scene, dressed in peaked caps and green uniforms, alert, efficient and good-tempered. The German policeman of today is a different being from the suspicious busybody of the Nazi era. By any standards, he is polite and noticeably friendly to a forlorn foreigner.

TWO aspects of Düsseldorf's traffic, however, defy successful regulation by the police. One is its noise, and the other is its disconcerting speed and unpredictability. Trolley cars, which the country's traffic experts still regard as the most economical form of urban transport, contribute a distinctive clank and rattle to the din. Police cars, flashing their blue lights and sounding their klaxons with a donkey's bray, are continuously on the move. The German motorist, while he does not overuse his horn, is an inveterate headlight-blinker both day and night, and he drives fast and furiously, which is one reason for the high accident rate. In some years since the war, the West Germans had the world's highest number of traffic deaths in proportion to the population. In 1964, for example, there were 16,500 dead and 446,000 injured in more than one million accidents in West Germany—almost twice as many injuries as there were in France.

Determination to be first in the race on the roads has had an impact on the motorists' manners. Not long ago a German law court even felt obliged to pronounce that "suggestive" head-tapping, with which one motorist deliberately mocks and infuriates another, was to be regarded as a punishable offense under the German penal code.

Apart from their sense of urgency, the Germans on the street look essentially commonplace. They dress neatly and unostentatiously. The youth may wear jeans and loud shirts in increasing numbers, but their elders remain soberly conservative. The women in a city like Düsseldorf are well dressed, although they do not seem to have much taste. Their hats are too often merely quaint, and their shoes tend to be clumsy. Perhaps their outstanding characteristics are their correct deportment in public (few German women smoke on the street), their tidiness and their obvious good health. The last quality applies to their menfolk, too. Germans as a rule are roughly handsome rather than appealing, bluntly vigorous rather than engagingly vital, and a bit lacking in superficial charm. They appear well scrubbed.

Like many other German cities, Düsseldorf looks very new. Its daily life is full, busy and normal. Indeed, the superficial normality of the Germans may be particularly startling to any visitor who knew prewar Germany from experience or hearsay. Under Hitler the picture of daily life was different. In those days, squads of soldiers seemed to be everlastingly on the march in their heavy boots. The brown-shirted *Sturmabteilung,* or Storm Troopers (S.A.), were always on the streets. Even the children wore uniforms.

DURING the Nazi era most impartial observers would probably have picked out three traits which then seemed peculiar to the Germans: arrogance, violence and aggressiveness. Their arrogance seemed to have been born out of a sense of their own strength—and a readiness to use that strength without regard for the feelings of others. Violence has been manifested in the Germans for a long time. In the 16th Century, for instance, one finds this statement on how to deal with the rebellious serf-peasants: "Therefore, let everyone who can, smite, slay, and stab [them], secretly or openly, remembering that nothing can be more poisonous, hurtful, or devilish than a rebel." These gory instructions—admittedly given in a gory era—came from none other than Martin Luther, the reformer of the German church.

In times of stress, the threat of violence has more than once risen to the surface in Germany. In the early days of the Weimar Republic following World War I, rabid German nationalists revived the *Femegerichte,* secret courts which condemned citizens to death *in absentia* and murdered them. These terroristic *Femegerichte* had been started by Germans in the Middle Ages as a weapon against the lawlessness of the time. In both periods of history they were unique in northern Europe.

German arrogance and violence reached a peak under the Nazis, who exploited these characteristics deliberately. The same is true of German aggressiveness, which found its extreme expression in the invasion of 15 neighboring countries by Hitler's armies between 1938 and 1944. Yet it would be unfair to tie these three labels—arrogance, violence and aggressiveness—to the necks of the Germans forever without making important qualifications. The first is that the Germans, from ancient times up to the modern era, have always possessed tremendous capacities for good as well as evil. Their courage, industriousness, orderliness and regard for family life have been exceptional. In their poets, philosophers, musicians and artists, they have produced men of brilliant attainments, and they have produced ordinary citizens who, if left to get on with the business of living, are as sober, honest and dependable as any in the world. To do nothing by halves is a German tradition. It may be that the good and bad qualities of the Germans seem more exaggerated than those of other peoples, and that Germans can also be more easily canalized and exploited.

IT may be that Germany has suffered to an unusual degree because of the facts of geography. Germany has always lacked natural frontiers in the west and, even more, in the east. This is what led in the past to the country's fear of encirclement by its neighbors. Placed as it is in the middle of Europe, Germany might have been a true heartland; instead it has too often felt that it was a juicy bone of contention between East and West.

Some of Germany's most striking natural features have not been entirely its own. The Rhine is popularly regarded as Germany's river, but only about half of it runs through German territory. The Danube rises in Germany but flows out of the country before completing a fifth of its journey to the Black Sea. The Elbe and Oder rise in Czechoslovakia. Germany's seaboard is broken in two by Denmark. The intrusion of the bastion of Bohemia (Czechoslovakia's western end) into southeastern Germany long interrupted the line of communication between Bavaria and Saxony. A lack of cohesion in Germany has always been emphasized by the rambling ridges of hills which separate the northern coastal plain from the valley of the Rhine and the Bavarian-Swabian plateau. Indeed, the most effective link that through the centuries bound Germany together was not geography but the German language. It was probably responsible for providing an essential basis for the "Germanness" of people so different in other respects as the Prussians, Swabians and Rhinelanders.

GERMANY has never had a real geographical center of gravity. By American standards most of the countries of western Europe are small, compact units, whose political, social and commercial life revolves around a capital city. But Berlin never became what London is to Britain or Paris to France. It was the capital of a united Germany for only 74 years, from 1871 to 1945. For nearly two centuries before that it was the capital of a purely north German and central European state, Prussia. Before that it was merely the chief city of the small Electorate of Brandenburg.

Even in the early years of this century the south and west Germans turned to their provincial capitals rather than to Berlin—to shop and trade, meet friends or go to the theater and opera. Munich, Kassel, Stuttgart, Dresden, Mainz—these places remained "capitals" in spirit long after Germany was unified by Prussia in 1871. Even around 1900 the members of the small grand-ducal court of Hesse-Darmstadt were disdainfully talking—in French—about *les Prusses,* their uncultured overlords in Berlin. And today the Rhineland Catholics still sometimes refer to "pagan" Berlin.

To be sure, Germany is a changed country since 1945, both geographically and in the apparent characteristics of its people. Prewar Germany, which straddled central Europe, no longer exists. Today the country is split into four parts—the Federal Republic in the west, the Communist-governed German Democratic Republic in the east, the split city of Berlin and the old Prussian provinces beyond the Oder-Neisse line (the boundary along the Oder and Neisse Rivers set by the 1945 Potsdam Conference) which are today occupied by and annexed to Poland and the Soviet Union. Roughly nine million Germans were expelled after World War II from these provinces—Pomerania, East Prussia, East Brandenburg and Silesia, with their plains, lakes, marshes and interminable pine forests. The chances of these provinces ever returning to Germany are remote, for three quarters of this area has been energetically resettled by the Poles, and much of what was once East Prussia has been turned into a military stronghold by the Soviet Union.

The meandering 800-mile border between East and West Germany is about the most unnatural frontier in the world. It does not merely split Germany between western Europe and the Communist bloc; often it cuts through the middle of villages, separating farmers from the land they used to cultivate and dividing friends and close relatives who until 1945 had lived all their lives next to each other.

Germany is unlucky in its soil as well as in its geography. Agriculturally it is poorer than most people outside Germany suppose. Until quite recent times, much of the North German Plain was swamp, forest and moorland. Prince von Bülow's description of pre-1914 Germany as "a well-tended garden" was an exaggeration —though German farmers have always done

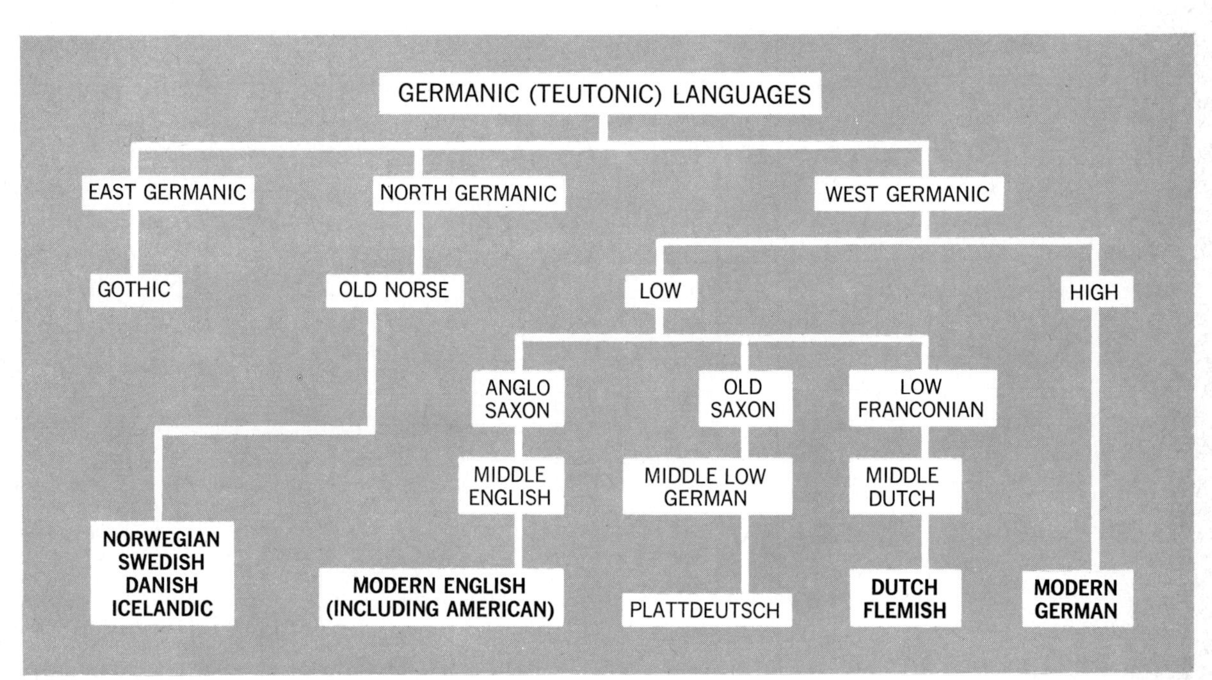

CLOSE KINSHIP between German and other modern languages is traced above. All of them, as well as a number of regional tongues—Afrikaans, Yiddish, Faroese, Frisian and Alsatian, to name only a few—derive through defunct dialects like Old Norse from still older tongues: the languages spoken by Germanic tribes who were settled in northern Europe before the birth of Christ. Pressed by invaders from Asia, some of these tribes later emigrated to the British Isles, where their language eventually evolved into English. All Teutonic tongues have, in addition, been enriched by influences from Latin and Latin's descendants, the Romance languages.

wonders with the existing cropland, managing to wrest a surprisingly high yield from the soil. Here and there the sandy soil grows good potatoes, as well as some of the best asparagus in Europe, but grain crops are difficult to wring from it. Much of Germany's soil, moreover, has been subjected to a strip system of farming, and the parceling-out of land to all male heirs in the past and the giving of land as a bride's dowry have further split up farm holdings. Much of the farmer's time has been wasted moving from one plot of ground to another, and his equipment has been subjected to excessive wear and tear.

PERHAPS the outstanding scenic feature of Germany is diversity. Follow a line across Germany from west to east, from the Dutch border near München Gladbach to Görlitz on the Neisse River, which today separates Germany from Poland. There is forest and heath between the Dutch border and München Gladbach, then a flat plain up to the valley of the Rhine. Beyond are the smoking coal and steel towns of the Ruhr, and beyond again the lakes and winding valleys of the Sauerland hills. Farther east are the steeper, thickly wooded slopes of the Hohe Meissner and the Reinhardswald, where the brothers Grimm discovered the castle of the Sleeping Beauty. Still farther east is the Thuringian Forest, where Goethe sat in rapt contemplation of the mists that swirled like a heavy veil over the mountains and wrote,

Uber allen Gipfeln
Ist Ruh,
In allen Wipfeln
Spürest du
Kaum einen Hauch. . . .

(Over every hillside is stillness. In every treetop you will sense—hardly a breath. . . .)

The west-east line leads on to Goethe's Weimar; to busy Saxony with its opencast coal fields and textile and chemical factories; to Dresden, one of the worst-bombed cities in Germany but still with more than a hint of its old charm; and to the small but bold peaks of Saxon Switzerland and the Polish frontier.

From north to south the country has just as much variety. Flensburg, only a few miles from Denmark, has a Danish neatness (and a minority of Danes among its inhabitants) and sits on its own low-banked fjord. Kiel is the haven of German yachtsmen, and Hamburg is one of the biggest seaports on the European mainland, with a sturdy sense of its own independence and a liberal-progressive tradition in politics. To the south are the moors of the Lüneburg Heath, then the uplands leading to the craggier escarpment of the Harz mountains and to the gloomy Brocken, the traditional mountaintop meeting place of the witches on Walpurgis Night in May.

Beyond Thuringia is the valley of the Main, fringed with vineyards, from which the picturesque *Romantische Strasse,* or "romantic road," leads southward through Rothenburg and Dinkelsbühl—perfectly preserved medieval towns—over the Bavarian plateau to the eight- and nine-thousand-foot peaks of the Alps.

THE land abounds in beauty spots: the Black Forest and the Bavarian highlands, the valleys of the Rhine, Neckar, Moselle and Weser Rivers and the lakes of Mecklenburg and Holstein. There are only a few corners—in the Hunsrück region and the Bavarian Forest hills, for instance—which are even comparatively free from the everlasting crowds, for there are six times as many cars on the German roads today as there were 10 years ago, and holidays away from home are now within nearly everyone's budget. The German countryside is as lovely as it ever was, especially in the spring, when the Rhine runs through acres of blossom, and in the autumn, when whole belts of wooded country are turned into skeins of gold and red and russet. But German towns have suffered both from the saturation bombing by the Allies during World War II and from hurried and "economy" building programs since. Few of the smaller towns survived unscathed, and every city suffered bitterly.

The old section of Frankfurt-on-Main, for example, has ceased to exist. Hamburg and Cologne lost more than half their buildings. The famed Cologne Cathedral was badly damaged, and the area around it was completely destroyed. By the late 1960s, however, most of the central areas of the large cities had been rebuilt, and modern buildings replaced the rubble left by bombing.

In *My Political Testament,* which he wrote during his last days, Adolf Hitler said, "Centuries will go by, but from the ruins of our cities and monuments, hatred of those ultimately responsible . . . will always grow anew." Certainly the psychological scars of war will need more time to heal, but it is doubtful whether Hitler's prophecy has much application today. The war he began changed at least one dominant theme in German history. The old fear of encirclement has been replaced, at least in what is today the West German Federal Republic, by a vivid awareness of the frontier between the western and Communist worlds. The division of Germany—however bitter for most Germans—has brought some 60 million West Germans into the camp of the western nations, probably for good. This change may gradually modify the national characteristics of the Germans, apart from showing them where their true interests lie.

WHEN Bismarck united Germany in 1871, he made sure that German strength and sense of purpose would counteract the imagined tendency of the country's neighbors to encircle it. His successors engendered within Germany the most expansive kind of counterpressure. The German *Dynamik,* or dynamic impulse, was the natural outcome of this urge. The *Dynamik* was a composite of many qualities, but perhaps the strongest was a restless energy. Germans even today work terribly hard, and business executives often suffer from "Manager's Disease," the steady deterioration of the overtaxed heart and arteries. Despite this, another aspect of *Dynamik* was—and is—animal good health. A pantheistic worship of sun and air has helped to give the Germans their fine physique.

But even in such simple things as energy and rude health, there are curious contradictions in the German character. Many of the stalwart young people undergo a marked change of attitude as the years pass, conforming to the German pattern in which everybody from early middle age onward worries excessively about health. More than any other Europeans, the Germans develop fads and fantasies about their physical condition. They take *Kneippkurs* by drenching themselves with icy water while standing in thickets; they trudge through the morning dew in bare feet; they discover that salt hardens the arteries, that coffee is bad for the heart, that drinks at mealtime ruin the digestion and that tea taxes the nerves. A young German is usually tough and vital; a middle-aged German is all too often fat and fearful.

ANOTHER facet of *Dynamik* is *Tüchtigkeit,* a word which implies a busy efficiency and which combines a belief in the job well done, a certain pedantry in its execution and a total inability to relax. Still another facet is described by the phrase *Ordnung muss sein* (there shall be order), the insistence on putting everyone and everything in the proper place. But along with German dynamism—and its cultivation and worship—have gone more dangerous characteristics than these. One was xenophobia: Germans of the Nazi era despised the Americans as a "mixed race," and they said much worse things about their European neighbors. Another was an irrational contempt for other nations—though this luckily is being evaporated today. Yet another was an overdeveloped self-pity, the product of wishing to be accepted and appreciated and not understanding why this did not happen.

The German urge to expand did not survive World War II. Its disappearance was due partly to the movement toward European unity, and to the cold war. It was also due partly to the division of Germany and to the realization on the part of most Germans that any renewal of military expansionism would not be tolerated by the U.S. and the Soviet Union. But German acceptance of a more modest place in the scheme of things is due at least as much to a new self-awareness. Thoughtful Germans are the first to admit today that "We have always tended to overdo everything" or "We have made the mistake of wanting everything or nothing." Self-awareness will not change the German character overnight, but it will season the German outlook.

In both outward appearance and inward thought, Germany—at least the greater part of it—has become a much more mundane place since 1945. The pursuit of prosperity has stamped itself on the German scene. In the towns there are almost no slums of the kind to be found in Britain and France. There is no visibly distinguishable working class. Germans are well dressed and well fed and they look decently contented. Most of the 9 million refugees and expellees from the former Prussian territories east of the Oder who now live in West Germany are impossible to distinguish from their fellow countrymen in their way of life.

YOUNG West Germans traditionally have been quiet, modest and unobtrusive, with the formal good manners of their fathers' generation but without their fathers' regimented orderliness. They have in the past shown less disposition than other young Europeans to throw their weight about. During the late 1960s, however, the same current of rebellion that electrified campuses in France and the U.S. was felt in West German universities. And although less than 10 per cent of West German youth ever reaches a university, these reverberations reached to the very highest echelons of the government.

German youth may seem a little dull and serious-minded, a bit over-anxious to get through their examinations and get on with the business of earning a living. But compared with their fathers, they are less bluntly assertive and far more open-minded. They have not accepted their fathers' views without question, largely because they identify their fathers with the Nazi disaster—and because their fathers realize this and are correspondingly more reticent. The young tend to listen hard and say little. They have an urge towards "Europeanism," and were the first young Europeans to demonstrate in favor of the removal of national frontiers. They feel essentially bound to the West; they are a rich promise for the future.

PROSPERITY has not touched the people of East Germany as much. To travel across the interzonal frontier is to move into a different world—a gray and sunless one. The East German roads are relatively empty, and the surface of even the *Autobahnen* (superhighways) is frequently cracked and pock-marked. The people wear drab clothes and poor-quality shoes. A large proportion of them are in uniform, for their People's Army—unlike the *Bundeswehr* in West Germany—does not hide itself away. There is no sense of lively bustle, no sign of enthusiasm. Above all, there are few smiles or sounds of laughter in the streets.

The joylessness of life in East Germany is underscored by the wartime ruins that have still not been cleared away, by the astonishingly high proportion of women doing comparatively heavy work and by the exorbitant prices of such consumer items as clothing and appliances. It is illustrated by the giant billboards with Communist slogans and pictures of Communist heroes, and by the pompous parades on May Day and on the anniversary of the Bolshevik October Revolution. Life in East Germany lacks natural colors. It is earnest and tinged with apprehension about what the dictatorial Communist regime may do.

The division of Germany may well continue to be the country's outstanding political and geographical feature. "The spectres which the Nazis invoked," an emigrated German Jew once wrote to a friend, "will haunt Germany, and all of us, forever. Luther unwittingly rent Germany into a northern [Protestant] and southern [Catholic] half. Hitler rent it into an eastern and western half. The Germans have nailed themselves to this cross." The seeming permanence of the present division of Germany leads one to wonder if the German people ever were an entity. Hitler's notions of a pure Aryan Germanic race can be consigned to the realm of mythology. North and east Germans may have generally conformed to his "ideal" Germanic type, with blond hair, blue eyes and big limbs. But plenty were dark and of medium build, and probably a majority of Bavarians and Rhinelanders have dark hair, brown eyes and round skulls.

The truth is that the Germans, like all other Europeans, have always been both racially and culturally mixed. There is plenty of Latin stock in the west and Slav blood in the east. Recently there have been significant changes in the population. One is the result of Hitler's campaign of anti-Semitism: the Jewish community in Germany has been reduced from more than half a million persons to around 30,000. The second change was produced by the World War II defeat: millions of refugees of German stock from east of the Oder-Neisse line have been spread over the Federal Republic, along with those who have come across the interzonal border from East Germany.

IN many Ruhr towns today about a third of the inhabitants are people who were born in other parts of Germany, perhaps as far east as Breslau and Königsberg, or even in the German-speaking "colonies" in the Baltic states and southeast Europe. Munich has been a minor cosmopolis ever since the immigration into Bavaria of Germans from every part of the Balkans and the arrival of other refugees from Communist oppression. This immense shake-up of population may eventually dilute German particularism, the old prejudice that was expressed in convictions such as that Saxons are sly, Prussians arrogant, Bavarians uncouth and Rhinelanders untrustworthy. It may make for a more integrated community in the long run.

It is fairly easy to make some forecasts about Germany. The West Germans will undoubtedly continue to concentrate their ingenuity and energy on material prosperity, with the creation of an influential, solid and respected international position as their logical goal. They will continue to treasure the relics of an older Germany—the Rhine castles and the baroque abbeys of the south, the Gothic churches, the art galleries and opera houses and the great artistic accomplishments. But the yardsticks of the new Germany will be the new homes built, the new factories, the skyscraper office blocks which are already going up, the new machinery in the fields and the spreading network of *Autobahnen*. The East Germans, on the other hand, must work as hard as possible merely to maintain a standard of living that is considerably lower. Their more labored progress is conditioned by the needs and the comparative austerity of the Communist bloc as a whole.

DIVISION means that the Germans have forfeited all claim to domination of eastern Europe. The birth rates in both East and West Germany are virtually static today. With so much territory in the east lost to Poland, Germany is now a far smaller place than it was in 1939 (when Berlin was farther from the eastern frontier at Memel than it was from the Rhine). In this smaller Germany there is no room for dreams and illusions, like Hitler's plan for a German nation of 250 million that would rule Europe from the English Channel to the Caucasus. Germans will in the future concentrate on well-being and survival.

The larger half of Germany, at least, is free—on the whole freer than it has ever been before. Within its borders German talent, fortitude and energy can flourish without hindrance. Its people are recapturing their ancient habits of orderly and purposeful living. The German in the Federal Republic no longer turns his back on the West. Yet this is only a compensatory thought to many Germans. For, failing a miracle, the two Germanies will grow further apart in the years ahead. In this lies the seed of fresh unrest, which could produce fresh signs of strain in the heart of Europe.

In the warm glow of sunset the twin spires of Cologne's 14th Century Gothic cathedral thrust high above the surrounding ancient city.

Timeless Verities in a Land of Turmoil

Few countries bear so tortured a history as Germany. For centuries its varied lands had only the cohesion of a common tongue; today its major parts are again sundered. Weary of unceasing change, of war and jackboots, Germany today looks inward to the timeless treasures of a lovely land: the exuberant art of Gothic and rococo churches, the majestic roll of river and field, the bright-eyed look of a new generation untouched by the horrors of the past.

THE STORIED RHINE *winds through Germany, hastening into gorges and wandering past rolling farmlands. It is Europe's busiest inland waterway*

SIGNAL TOWER on the Rhine warns of oncoming vessels. Opposite rears the rock of the Lorelei, the golden maiden whose siren song lured medieval rivermen to destruction.

SPECTACULAR VISTA unfolds from left-bank heights as the Rhine turns ponderously past the farm village of Filzen. In the right background is the walled town of Boppard.

VALLEY CHAPEL nestled in the vineyards (*left*) near Lorchhausen is attended by worshipers underneath multicolored umbrellas on a rainy fall Sunday.

HILLSIDE LIFT at Assmannshausen affords a sweeping view of the Rhine and, at the summit, a look at a spot where pirates were once hanged.

GOLDEN FIELD of vines (*below*) near Bacharach is harvested by peasant women. By legend, wine making in the Rhineland began with Charlemagne.

DEVOTIONAL DRAMA *is presented once a decade in Oberammergau*

MAMMOTH STAGE at Oberammergau is crowded as townsfolk re-enact the drama of Christ's final days on earth. First offered in 1634 in gratitude for deliverance from a virulent plague, the Passion play is the most renowned religious spectacle in Europe. It drew almost half a million spectators during the summer of 1960.

In triumphant illusion a heavenly host swirls from the ceiling of the 18th Century church of Zwiefalten in Swabia. German love of the rococo flowered in the churches of the south.

MUSIC AND FOOD *are a part of life in Bavaria*

OPERA HOUSE, the National Theater of Munich was restored by 1963. The city spends large sums on cultural activities.

BEAMING HOST, the late Alfred Walterspiel created Crepes Barbara (*left*) and other delicacies of his Munich restaurant.

THE OPULENT LIFE *is available to increasing numbers*

GIRLS IN A GARDEN, Ingrid and Ellen Farnsteiner (*opposite*), daughters of a wealthy Munich family, compare their new afternoon frocks at a Bavarian resort.

MAID IN A SUBURB tends children in the prosperous Othmarschen section outside Hamburg. The prices of homes in this neighborhood run to $62,000 and up.

In the cozy fellowship Germans call "Gemütlichkeit," Bavarians quaff an evening away in Munich's ancient Hofbräuhaus. Beer halls

are found everywhere in Germany, but nowhere in such number as in Bavaria, where per capita consumption exceeds 200 quarts a year.

Conqueror of Romans, the barbarian chief Arminius is shown in an old painting being greeted in triumph after defeating an imperial

The Unresolved Quest for Unity

2

army in the Teutoburg Forest in 9 A.D. After this battle, Rome never again made serious efforts to colonize Germany beyond the Rhine.

THE division of Germany after 1945 into eastern and western halves seems abnormal today. Yet not so long ago, there were many Germans who had been born at a time when the country was disunited—as it had been for centuries. Unity came in 1871 with Otto von Bismarck, who guided his country with a policy of "blood and iron" and with a blend of astuteness, opportunism and deceit that his successors may have envied but were unable to emulate. In the long span of time, Germany's history has been one of endless division.

"This country," said André François-Poncet, who served as French High Commissioner in Germany from 1949 to 1955, "is open to all the winds of the continent." It always has been. One way to visualize this is to think of western Europe as a funnel, with its wide end in eastern Europe and its outlet pointing toward Spain or Portugal. One thrust of population after another has forced its way into this funnel. What is called Germany today lay across the path of nearly every invasion originating in the tremendous open areas of the East—of the earliest Teutonic tribes, the Slavs and the Magyars, among others. People on the periphery of the funnel—in Britain, Spain, France and Scandinavia—had a better chance of settling down and thus more opportunity to develop a distinct national identity. The people of Germany had far less chance of doing so.

GLACIAL sheets, which covered a large part of Europe in the ice age, left a bleak, forbidding country south of the Baltic Sea. This country bequeathed few relics of that twilight past, apart from the skull of the Steinheim man, a precursor of the Neanderthal man and among the first *Homo sapiens*, who lived 250,000 years ago. Later, Celtic and Teutonic tribes and other peoples came from various parts of Europe and Asia, and settled in the forests and on the plains. In the days of Rome's glory Germany stood on the fringe of history. The Romans established trading posts far beyond the Rhine; it was from them that much of the information came for the historian Tacitus' *Germania*, the first clear historical account of the Germanic tribes. Roman engineers built a *limes*, or fortified road, that stretched from the Danube near Regensburg to the Rhine near Coblenz, and the Romans left cultural traces which may still show in the differences between north and south Germany.

Not a great deal remains in Germany of what the Romans built—and the Romans built well, and built much. There are pieces of Roman pavements in Cologne, Coblenz and Mainz; Roman weapons and drinking vessels are still being dug out of the ground of the Palatinate and at a new-found Roman site in the Ruhr. But among German towns, Trier alone has preserved considerable Roman remains. Only once did the Romans make a serious effort to extend their empire into the interior. In the year 9 A.D. General Publius Quintilius Varus and his legions, 20,000 strong, advanced toward the river Weser and were routed by the Cherusci, under Arminius (Hermann). A huge monument stands today on the slopes of the Teutoburg hills to commemorate this victory of the Germanic tribes over Roman civilization.

These and other Germanic tribes poured into western Europe when the Roman Empire began to collapse. Goths and Vandals flooded into Spain and Italy, Franks into France, and Angles, Saxons and Jutes into Britain. Behind them a new pressure of population was pushing westward. The Slavic Prussians arrived on the shores of the Baltic, and in the Fifth Century the Huns under Attila forced their way through Germany and were only beaten on the plains of northern France. Western Europe was slow to set up a counterpressure to the east. But around 800 the Emperor Charlemagne—the Germans claim him for their own and call him "Karl der Grosse"—fought a series of campaigns which established western control of Germany up to the river Elbe.

Here was Germany's first chance for coherent development. Charlemagne brought Christianity with him to the heathen Saxons, who accepted it only under compulsion. Elsewhere the Christian bishoprics, which had been established earlier by foreign missionaries, were strengthened, and new ones were instituted. Forests were cleared, roads and bridges built. Arts and letters flourished, a school system was set up and the earlier tribal way of life declined. Charlemagne made his capital at Aachen (Aix-la-Chapelle), where his bones still rest.

AFTER Charlemagne's son and successor, Louis the Pious, died in 840, the revived Roman Empire was split into three parts by the Treaty of Verdun (843). This was another turning point in German history. The German kingdom faced about, turning eastward in order to beat back the Slavs and Magyars. But the Germans did not drop their claim to Charlemagne's heritage. In 962 a Saxon, Otto, accepted the imperial crown, thus beginning what was later called the Holy Roman Empire.

The connection between Germany and Rome was a fatal one. It involved Germany's rulers in Italian affairs and in quarrels with the papacy; a famous quarrel came to a climax at Canossa, where in 1077 Emperor Henry IV waited barefoot in the snow for three days until the pope would receive him. Such complications made the consolidation of a German state difficult. In the 11th and 12th Centuries, to be sure, Germany seemed no unluckier than other European countries. England was invaded by the Normans; few people would have guessed that this was the last time that a foreign army would set foot on English soil. The French monarchy was barely establishing itself in Paris. The Spaniards were fighting for their existence against the Moslems.

THERE were hopeful signs in Germany as well. Towns like Nuremberg, Frankfurt and Augsburg, lying on trade routes that connected northern Europe with Italy and Constantinople, were becoming centers of craftsmanship and commerce. The north German towns of Hamburg and Bremen were forming their own governments, trading and constructing fortifications. Not only was the eastern frontier being held, but the Church was encouraging expansion eastward. Cistercian monks were in the vanguard of settlers that thrust into Brandenburg and Silesia, set up monasteries, built villages in place of the Slavic encampments and stimulated the growth of an orderly society. By the 13th Century the Germans were established as far east as the Oder.

Although there were some signs of political stability and centralization in 12th and 13th Century Germany, permanent institutions did not grow from them. The dynasties of the Guelphs (the dukes of Saxony and Bavaria) and the Hohenstaufens, or Ghibellines (from Waiblingen, a village owned by the powerful Hohenstaufen family), fought for supremacy, carving segments from each other's domains and installing princes friendly to their interests. Political divisions, moreover, went much further than those between emperor and dukes. The nobility was becoming increasingly independent, and a new sense of "particularism" was arising in the country.

One emperor, Frederick Barbarossa (Redbeard), who was related to both Guelphs and Ghibellines, ruled the Holy Roman Empire for 38 years. An energetic empire builder and administrative reformer, he had no fixed capital, spent most of his life on the move and eventually drowned in the icy waters of a river of Asia Minor. He left behind the legend that he is still sleeping in a cave in the Kyffhäuser mountains, his beard growing through a wooden table and down to the ground. When the raven's croak is heard on these hills, so one legend runs, Barbarossa will awake, take up his spear and save his people.

Frederick II, who came soon afterward, legally recognized the autonomy of the German princes, an act sealed in the famed Golden Bull of 1356. Up to the 16th Century Germany's history was one of cleavage between warring groups. In 1517 came a new kind of division. On October 31 of that year, Martin Luther, a stern-minded Catholic priest, nailed to the door of Wittenberg's church his 95 theses attacking the Roman Church. Three years later, by Wittenberg's Elster gate, he burned a papal message threatening to excommunicate him. Luther produced a religious cleavage—roughly, the preponderantly Protestant German north against the mainly Catholic south.

Luther was a genuine reformer, who translated the Bible from Greek and Hebrew into German and who preached the idea of "protesting" church abuses and spiritual corruption, and exalting Christian virtue and simplicity. For a while he seemed to be paving the way for the creation of a Protestant north German state that would stretch from Aachen to the river Oder and from the Baltic to the river Main.

BUT the papacy had no intention of giving up Germany. The Catholic Counter Reformation, stemming from many sources, swept through many countries and eventually reached western Germany. In 1618 the Thirty Years' War broke out with the revolt of the Bohemian nobles. In it the Catholic emperor, Ferdinand II, fought west and north German Protestantism; the north Germans were defended by Denmark, Sweden and France in the interests of politics. The religious issue gradually became submerged in a war against the power of the Habsburgs. It was the most destructive period in all German history. Most European nations were left with either predominant Protestant majorities (Britain, Holland and Sweden, among others) or Catholic ones (France, Italy, Austria). But at the end of the Thirty Years' War Germany was still religiously split down the middle, with a bare majority of its inhabitants adhering to Lutheranism. Its population had sunk from approximately 21 to 13 million, and some Germans were reduced to cannibalism. Its cities had declined in wealth and power. And the Treaty of Westphalia, which ended the war in 1648, left more than 300 separate units of government in Germany.

Germans often say they are not responsible for their own country's history. As far as the Thirty Years' War is concerned, there is evidence on their side. Spanish armies ravaged central Germany. The Danes invaded south into Brunswick. Catholic France intervened on the Rhine in order to keep the Austrian House of Habsburg from ruling the German north. The Swedish king marched through the north and was killed in battle near Leipzig. All sense of order, unity and purpose disappeared. It looked as if the fragmentation of Germany would last indefinitely.

AT the end of the 17th and beginning of the 18th Centuries the idea of a German "nation" was still persisting, but the old empire was impotent. Bavaria was one of several "electorates," each with a fiercely local patriotism. Hanover was linked with England in 1714, when its own Georg Ludwig became King George I of England. Many cities were independent. So were states such as Mecklenburg, Hesse-Darmstadt and Württemberg, which maintained courts like the ones the 20th Century British poet Siegfried Sassoon described as "the fairy-tale of flunkeydom." From Hesse-Cassel came much of the manpower for the English armies, and Hessian and other German regiments were dispatched to America to fight for England in the War of Independence.

Some Germans still revered the tradition of a Germanic Holy Roman Empire. For them the Habsburg realm of Austria must have appeared the only power which might be strong enough to lead Germany out of its divisive existence and into a major role in European affairs. But Austria's traditions were dynastic and its interests were increasingly focused on the countries around the Danube. Allied by royal marriage with Spain, Austria held parts of the Low Countries and Italy. It had the mental agility but not the physical power to unite Germany against French resistance and German small-state inertia. And it was becoming predominantly a Central European power rather than a German one.

THERE was, however, one state which would eventually unite Germany. That was Prussia. Before the late 18th Century no one outside Prussia's own borders—and very few people within them—would have guessed this of a kingdom which was an amalgam of the Electorate of Brandenburg, the former Duchy of Prussia and some miscellaneous territories in the west. Up to about 1000 A.D. the territories which eventually became the eastern part of Prussia had been held by Slavic and Baltic tribes. Early in the 13th Century the Order of Teutonic Knights—founded during the Third Crusade to care for the poor, sick and wounded and to drive the infidel from the Holy Land—had been invited by the Poles to lead a crusade against the heathen Prussian tribesmen. Members of the order were knights, priests and lay brothers, bound by a vow of chastity and a military oath, and they were great builders of castles as they pushed eastward during the 13th and 14th Centuries. They virtually exterminated the Prussian tribesmen, and they made East Prussia a German province. Later the order fought countless battles against the Poles. It had a real sense of mission; German historians, in later years, were inclined to regard it as the vanguard of the "master race" which was destined to conquer eastern Europe.

The order retained its power into the 16th Century, and in 1511 a south German prince of the Hohenzollern family, Albert, became its Grand Master. During the Protestant Reformation he secularized the order and declared its lands to be his personal dukedom. When the male line of his family died out, less than a century later, a daughter of his ducal house, Anne, married the Electoral Prince of Brandenburg. East Prussia and Brandenburg, which had become a Hohenzollern possession in the early 15th Century, formed the core of the future Kingdom of Prussia.

THE crusading zeal of the Teutonic Knights gave way to the political ambitions of the Hohenzollerns. The Prussian townspeople were thrifty, and their peasants were disciplined and loyal to the *Junker* class of landlords. The new Kingdom of Prussia, which was officially founded in 1701, was the Sparta of northern Europe. It became a European power of consequence when the ambitious and dynamic Frederick the Great, who ruled from 1740 to 1786, seized Silesia from the Austrian empress, Maria Theresa, successfully resisted Austria, France and Russia during the Seven Years' War, and joined in the First Partition of Poland in 1772, by which he acquired western Prussia.

Frederick was brave if severe, a brilliant if lucky general. His conquests almost doubled the area of Prussia. He built Sans Souci Palace at Potsdam and invited philosophers, poets and architects to his court. But his and Prussia's strength was founded on a regular army which grew to 200,000—huge for those days—and on the "Prussian virtues" of courage, discipline, frugality and hard work. The Prussian state was sustained by two institutions, the army and the civil service—both dominated by the *Junker* landholding class.

Prussia was crushed by Napoleon in 1806-1807, but paradoxically Napoleon gave the conquered kingdom the chance to lead Germany. He swept away scores of small principalities. More important, he destroyed once and for all the concept of a Germanic Holy Roman Empire. The 1815 Congress of Vienna, by reducing the number of German states from two hundred-odd to 39, confirmed his work. Prussia gained several territories, including the Rhineland, whose immense deposits of coal have helped make the Ruhr one of the most concentrated industrial areas in the world.

What finally made Prussia's subsequent rise to German leadership logical was the failure of German liberalism in the 19th Century. German liberalism was unable to follow through its many constructive ideas for a future united Germany. In 1848—the year of revolutions in Europe—German liberals called for a free press, trial by jury, a national militia and a German parliament. The liberals wanted the old, outworn Federal Diet of German states reformed in order to open the way for true German unification. It looked as if they might succeed when a National Assembly was convened in Frankfurt in May 1848, and a written constitution for Germany was drawn up. If this constitution had been implemented and enforced, it would have realized liberal aims. A federation of German states, established as a constitutional monarchy under the King of Prussia and pledged to progress toward democratic forms, would have been the result.

THE 1848 Revolution in Germany failed for a multitude of reasons. The reformers were themselves not united. The liberals and the radicals did not cooperate. Several months were frittered away in somewhat aimless discussions. Meanwhile, counter-revolution was sweeping through Austria, still the most powerful single German state, and gaining strength in Prussia. In July the revolution was finally put down in Prague and Bohemia, and in October in Vienna. Prussia was the last hope of the liberals. But the Prussian government rejected the Frankfurt Constitution, the King of Prussia informing a deputation from the assembly that he would never stoop "to pick up a crown out of the gutter."

Both Austria and Prussia reverted to their own conservative traditions. This doomed the liberal revolution, and the well-to-do middle class decided to back the established order once again and put its progressive notions into cold storage. Many disillusioned liberals and radicals emigrated to America. After such bright promise, the German National Assembly had a sadly short life. The German people, it has been said, "greeted it like a Goddess of Liberty, and a year later discharged it like a prostitute." They might have accepted democratic progress in 1848; the dominance of Austria and Prussia ensured that their next fleeting chance to achieve democracy would not come until 1919, after a lost war that made political liberty look far less important than the restoration of German material strength.

WHEN Prussia turned against the 1848 Revolution, one contemporary writer, Ludwig Simon, addressed his countrymen by saying, "If you allow yourselves to be conquered by Prussia, you will preserve in Germany the peace of the grave and the order of the churchyard." German liberals may still have hoped for more from Prussia than from ultraconservative Austria. Their hopes were doomed by the rise of Otto von Bismarck, a count (later prince) from a *Junker* family of Brandenburg. Only 33 at the time of the 1848 Revolution and brimming with energy and ideas, Bismarck was horrified (though impressed) by the Revolution. A promising member of the Prussian parliament, he decided that the unification of all German-speaking peoples was no more than a dream. He chose instead to work for the unification of Germany—without the Austrian Empire—under Prussian leadership.

He believed in power, and his beliefs found their way into Prussian policies. "Great crises," he once wrote, "are the very weather which stimulates Prussia's growth, if we turn them to our account fearlessly and, maybe, very recklessly." And on another occasion: "The importance of a state is measured by the number of soldiers it can put into the field of battle. . . . It is the destiny of the weak to be devoured by the strong."

With consummate finesse Bismarck waged three successive wars, in 1864, 1866 and 1870. He made no secret of his belief that Prussia would have to fight wars in order to unify Germany. For the first, he depicted Denmark as a foreign body on German soil because it held part of the provinces of Schleswig and Holstein. For the second, he claimed that Austria was the archexponent of reaction. Finally, in 1870, France became the national enemy.

Bismarck won his three wars. With an eye to the future, he decided against imposing a hard peace on Austria. As a result he was able to ensure Austrian neutrality during the Franco-Prussian War of 1870, and to gain Austrian friendship which led to a later alliance. From France he took Alsace and most of Lorraine, also forcing the French to pay an indemnity of one billion dollars, a gigantic sum in those days. The French paid off their debt, but they never forgave the annexation of French territory. At the end of the Franco-Prussian War, the German Empire was proclaimed in the Hall of Mirrors at Versailles, once the palace of the French kings.

GERMANS still claim that, beginning in the time of Bismarck, other European powers started a stealthy *Einkreisung*, or encirclement, of their country and that this forced them into counterpressure, thereby creating the explosive situation which brought about World War I. It can be more cogently argued that Bismarck's successors—he ceased to be Chancellor in 1890—were power-conscious and power-hungry, but lacked his diplomatic finesse and knowledge that Germany needed friends (Bismarck had befriended Russia and was careful in his dealings with England).

His successors were a poor lot. They had few constructive ideas and tended to knuckle under to Kaiser Wilhelm II, who ascended the throne in 1888 and whose sporadic political influence was rooted in ambition, bluster and muddled well-meaning. The Kaiser thought in grand terms of a world empire, although the latter-day German Empire never consisted of

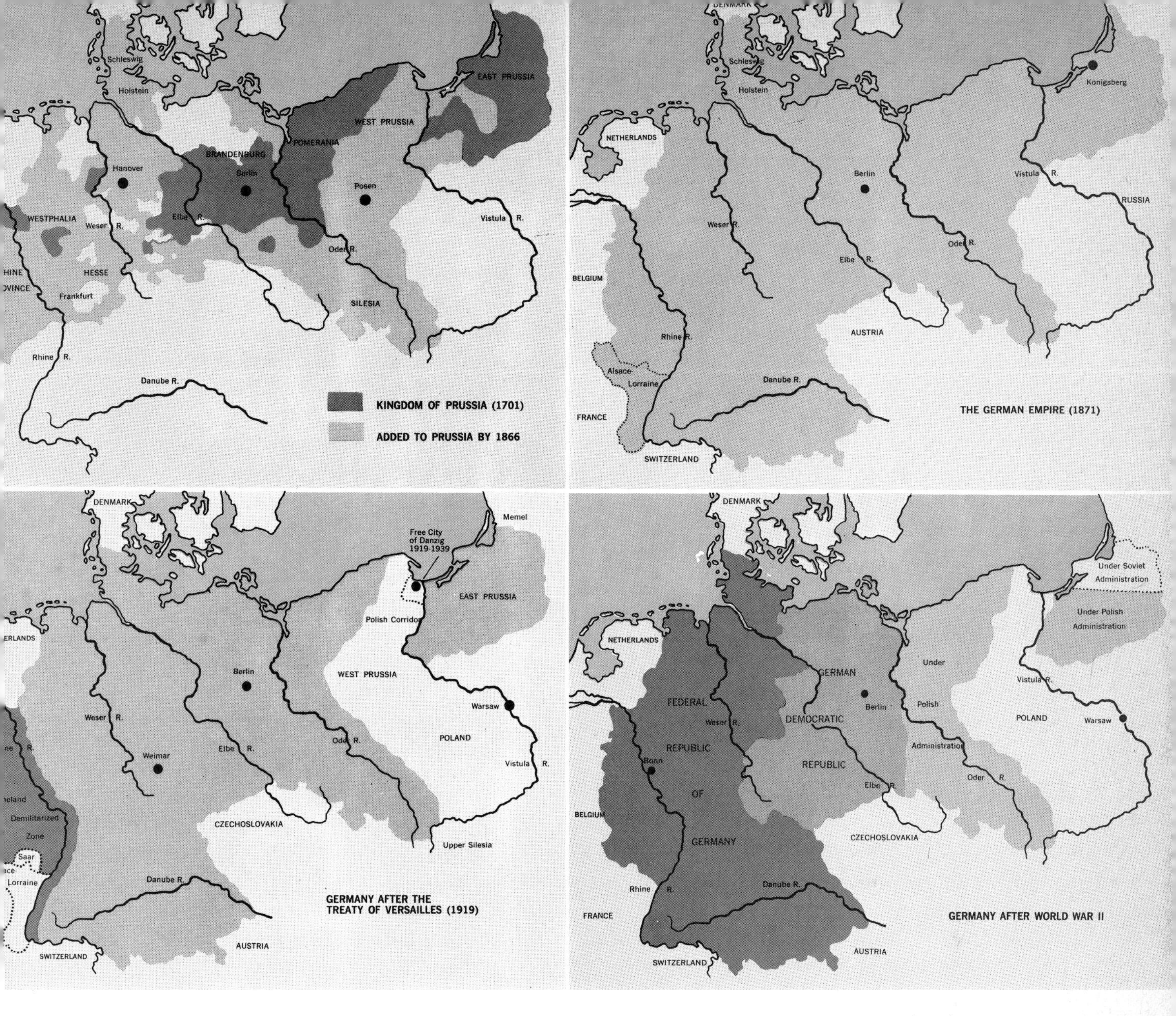

CHANGING SHAPE of Prussia and Germany over 245 years is shown above. Not counting territories annexed before and during World War II, Germany was at its largest between 1871 and 1914. At Versailles (1919) it lost big areas to France and Poland. In 1945 it lost what in 1866 had been the whole eastern half of Prussia.

more than four African territories—Togoland, the Cameroons, German East Africa (Tanganyika and Ruanda-Urundi) and German South-West Africa—and a number of islands in the Pacific. His dream coincided with the development in Germany of a Navy League, a Colonial Society and a strong fleet which threatened Britain, and with plans for a Berlin-Baghdad railway and a German domain in the East.

Despite his sentimental ties with England —Queen Victoria was his grandmother—Kaiser Wilhelm threatened to intervene against British interests in South Africa. When a crisis arose over China, he told his troops to behave "like the Huns" and strike terror into the hearts of their foes. The German government intervened in Morocco. The Chief of the General Staff, Alfred von Schlieffen, was encouraged to develop his plan for a "right hook" through the Low Countries in the next war with France—no matter that Belgium's neutrality was guaranteed by England. Germany's entry into World War I began with just this move.

The Germans fought the war with immense courage and enthusiasm. In 1914 they marched with high hopes and with an intense belief in the rightness of Germany's cause—a Germany proud, confident and brought up in the spirit of self-sacrifice to the state. Even the growing Social Democrats supported the war. The German armies battered Russia to defeat by 1917, and in the spring of 1918 they severely damaged the armies of a united western alliance—which now included the United States. German military genius achieved epic victories—only to lose the war.

Germany was given a hard peace. The Treaty of Versailles deprived Germany of its colonies, created the Polish Corridor to Danzig between East Prussia and the rest of Germany and imposed heavy financial reparations. Even Winston Churchill later called the Versailles economic clauses "malignant and silly."

LOOKING back on Versailles, one can easily understand the sense of outrage on the part of the victor nations, who, as they saw it, had saved Europe from conquest by a starkly militaristic state that utterly disregarded the feelings of its neighbors. This sense of outrage by the Allies unwittingly eroded the Weimar Republic, which was set up in 1919 and which allowed itself to be taken over by Adolf Hitler in 1933.

For their part, the Germans never overcame the sourness which the peace engendered in them. They invented the myth of the "stab in the back" at home, with only the 1917 and 1918 minor naval mutinies in Kiel as "evidence"; and the first President of the Weimar Republic, Friedrich Ebert, welcomed the homecoming German armies with the statement, "I salute you, on your return undefeated from the field of battle." Resentment against the victors meant that a great many Germans no longer felt that they belonged to the West. This made it supremely difficult for the Weimar Republic to develop a rational republican tradition. The new government was identified with defeat, and German nationalists in particular violently opposed what was called the "policy of fulfillment"—meaning admission that the war had been lost and acceptance of the conditions imposed by the victors.

Yet for a while the Weimar Republic seemed to have a good chance of survival. The Locarno Pacts, signed in 1925 between Germany and the western powers, opened the way for Germany's entrance into the League of Nations. The victor nations agreed to evacuate the Rhineland, which had been occupied at the end of the war as a guarantee against future German armed aggression in Europe. The heavy financial reparations imposed on Germany were modified by the Dawes and Young Plans, which were drawn up by Americans and sponsored by the Allies, and American money began to flow into the country.

After a disastrous inflation of the currency, which reached its height in 1923, the country's finances were put onto a firm footing again, chiefly by Dr. Hjalmar Schacht, who later became Adolf Hitler's financial adviser. Despite nationalist attempts to seize power—Hitler's Munich *Putsch* of 1923 was only one of several—the policy of fulfillment appeared to be succeeding up to 1929. Germans who lived during those first 10 postwar years talked of them afterwards as a time full of dangerous strains, yet full too of hope and promise—a springtime of the spirit.

BUT many Germans after 1919 had always wanted to "win their way back," to "restore the national honor" and to make their country great again—great in the sense of material power and armed might. Three events of 1929 played into their hands. First, Gustav Stresemann, the foreign minister who had worked unceasingly for an understanding with the victor nations, died of a series of strokes brought on by overwork. His death was a heavy setback to the sponsors of the policy of fulfillment. Second, the Wall Street crisis in the United States shook the whole economic fabric of Europe, and Germany was hit worst of all the continental countries. By 1933 unemployment was above eight million. Finally, the Nazi party under Hitler stepped up its drive for power.

The Nazi party, whose name came from the German pronunciation of the first letters of "National Socialist," had been well-nigh forgotten after the 1923 *Putsch*. Hitler was imprisoned in Landsberg jail for almost nine months. In the 1928 elections the Nazis secured only 12 out of 491 seats in the *Reichstag*, or parliament. They polled less than a million votes, while the Social Democrats, who had been the mainstay of most coalition cabinets since 1919, polled over nine million. But the eventual triumph of the Nazis was foreshadowed in the 1930 elections, when their vote rose to nearly six and a half million and their seats to 107.

PERHAPS the German people would not have rejected both the Treaty of Versailles and democratic rule if they had been guaranteed prosperity. As it was, the Nazis made a tremendous appeal to a discontented people with their insistence on order and discipline, their promise of economic rejuvenation, their reliance on their own militarily trained Storm Troopers and their demands for the revision of the Treaty of Versailles and the return of Danzig, the Polish Corridor and other lost territories. Hitler won the support of the extreme right-wing Nationalist party, and at least the tacit connivance of the *Reichswehr*, or German regular army.

The Weimar Republic disintegrated because, among other things, the democratic parties were too numerous and failed to combine against Hitler. But, although the Nazis obtained less than 44 per cent of the votes in the March 1933 election and seized power only after a campaign of intimidation and repression, they capitalized on German discontent. It was primarily discontent which induced the great majority of Germans to entrust their destinies to Hitler in 1933. It is an inescapable fact that Hitler, once he had helped to restore the country's economic position and to fulfill his boasts in the field of foreign policy, commanded immense popular support. Criticism of his regime may have been brutally stifled but it was also very limited.

In 1935 Hitler rearmed in violation of the Versailles limitations on German arms. He then remilitarized the Rhineland, thereby flouting both the Treaty of Versailles and the Locarno Pacts. In March 1938, he moved into Austria, with the connivance of the fanatical Austrian Nazi party. In September of the same year, he secured the annexation of the predominantly German-speaking areas of Czechoslovakia, by threatening to use military force and by taking advantage of the weakness and indecision of Britain and France. In March 1939, he occupied the whole of Czechoslovakia. He attacked Poland only six months later.

World War II was Germany's renewed challenge to western civilization. For in 1939, in a last-minute alliance with the Communists, the Germans called in Russia to underwrite their conquest of Poland. The alliance enabled them to overrun the friendly neutral countries of Denmark, Norway, Holland, Belgium and Luxembourg, and to wreak revenge on France. Hitler meant, of course, to destroy Russia in its turn; it is a remarkable reflection on Stalin's gullibility at the time that he refused to believe this. He had been lulled into a false sense of security. Hitler handed him the eastern half of Poland, the Baltic states and part of Rumania, and stood by while he attacked Finland.

THEN, in an act which marked a great turning point in his fortunes, Hitler turned on his ally and attacked the Soviet Union in June of 1941. By so doing he began a chain of events which brought the Red Army into the heart of Europe. He destroyed Prussia, whose name has since been rubbed off the map. He left behind him a sharply divided Germany, his final legacy to his people.

The lasting division is in many ways more bitter to the Germans than defeat. It is an unnatural state for a great people who, with more time, patience and common sense, could have given so much to Europe.

MASTERFUL CHANCELLOR, Otto von Bismarck forged the modern German state. This photograph was taken in 1871, the year the new empire was proclaimed.

Fleeting Glories of Empire

HEADSTRONG KAISER, Wilhelm II (*left*) dismissed Bismarck in 1890 and assumed a wider role for himself in affairs of state. He died an exile in Holland in 1941.

In the closing years of the 19th Century, a new Germany emerged. One by one, expansionist Prussia had brought the independent states of the disunited land under its control. Grandiloquently, the new empire ruled by the Hohenzollern family was proclaimed, a Teutonic revival of the long-dead empire of Charlemagne. But imperial days were few. The empire was tumbled by defeat in World War I. Out of its ashes rose the hapless Weimar Republic, then the grandiose Third Reich of Adolf Hitler. His "Thousand-Year" Empire lasted 12 years.

FALLEN STAGS are inspected (*above*) in 1913 by Kaiser Wilhelm II (*foreground*) and his hunting partner, Archduke Franz Ferdinand of Austria (*far left*). Within five years both hunters had fallen—Franz Ferdinand assassinated in 1914 (the event precipitating World War I), the Kaiser forced to abdicate on Germany's defeat in 1918.

OLD COMRADES, Brown Shirts gather with the Führer (*center, rear*) in 1932. First of the Nazi strong-arm squads, the Brown Shirts lost influence two years later when Hitler ordered the execution of most of their top leaders.

PARTY SHRINE, the Munich beer hall (*opposite*) which was the party's first office displays Nazi insignia in this 1937 picture. As an army corporal in 1919, Hitler was sent to investigate the party here, but instead joined it.

COURTESY CALL is paid by Hitler in 1933 (*left*) on Germany's president, Paul von Hindenburg, who had appointed him chancellor that year. Hindenburg's death in 1934 removed a final threat to Nazi rule of Germany.

HITLER'S RISE *swiftly toppled the troubled Weimar Republic*

NSDAP

ADULATION *for the Führer was a keynote of the Nazis' middle years*

MASSED THOUSANDS assemble *(opposite)* in Hitler's honor at Bückeburg in 1937. Elaborately organized, such rallies featured group pledges of fealty to the Führer.

HIGH GLEE overtakes Hitler as young people break ranks to greet him on his arrival at Bückeburg. All German children were required to enroll in Hitler youth groups.

GRIM DEPUTIES to the Nazi *Reichstag* salute Hitler (*second from left, bottom row*) after a 1939 anti-U.S. speech in Berlin's Kroll Opera House. *Reichstag* sessions were held here after the mysterious burning of the original *Reichstag* building in 1933. It is believed that the Nazis fired it in an effort to discredit German Communists.

AFFABLE HITLER is lionized (*right*) by Nazi wives at a 1939 party. He gave up such affairs when the war's tide turned against Germany.

THE FUHRER'S WORLD *was bright in the high days when nations waited fearfully on his word*

VICTORIES *were fleeting for Hitler's Reich*

DOOMED MISSION found British Prime Minister Neville Chamberlain (*second from right, above*) in Munich in 1938 to ensure "peace in our time."

BLACK HOUR, France's 1940 defeat brought the Führer (*second from left*) to the Compiègne railroad car in which Germany capitulated in 1918.

HEAVY ARMS rolled in front of Hitler on his 50th birthday in 1939 (*right*). Six years later he lay dead by his own hand in besieged Berlin.

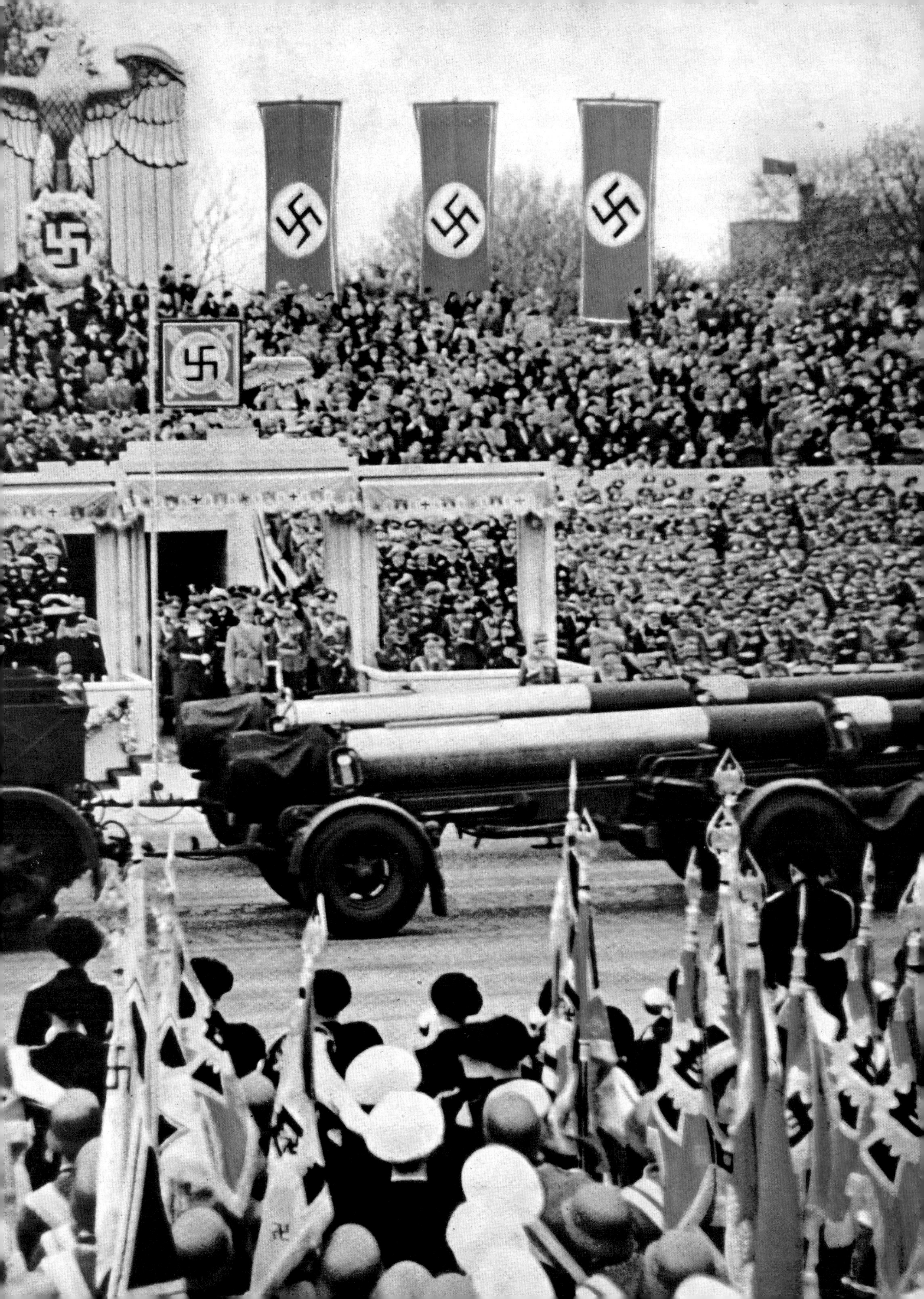

VISITING QUEEN, Elizabeth of Britain attends a Berlin reception with German leaders on a 1965 trip. Her visit was the first by a ruling British monarch since 1909.

3

Construction of a Stable State

WHEN Germany was divided following World War II, the country's unified political system was broken up into three parts. Today a Communist dictatorship holds sway over the German Democratic Republic, the former Soviet zone now generally referred to as East Germany. A modified occupation system, in which Britain, France and the United States retain some rights, survives despite Soviet harassment in West Berlin. And in the Federal or West German Republic, democratic self-government has functioned smoothly since the creation of a federal parliament in 1949. The three systems of government are so different—in the cases of the Federal Republic and East Germany, sharply different—that they must be discussed separately. This chapter is concerned with the Federal Republic.

In countries like the United States and Britain which have a durable thread of continuity running through their histories, the idea of a nation having to make a fresh start is foreign. But Germany had to do just this in 1945, thanks to the legacy that Hitler gave the nation. Hitler had long held a fatalistic belief in the *Götterdämmerung*, or "Twilight of the Gods," a concept dramatized by Richard Wagner, the 19th Century German composer. According to this idea, the defeat of gods and heroes presupposed total collapse and self-annihilation. While the Reich Chancellery in Berlin was burning in April 1945 and enemy forces were advancing into the last unconquered corners of the land, Hitler made little attempt to save anything of—or for—his country, though he did appoint a caretaker government before he died.

The last-ditch battle which he forced the German people to fight appeared to have wrecked the country. All the larger cities were in ruins. Some three million men had been marched off to Allied prison camps. Nearly three million servicemen had died or were missing. There was a growing—eventually a desperate—food shortage. Organs of the Nazi government had ceased to function and were taken over by the occupying powers. Germany was divided into four zones of occupation: French, British, American and Russian. In the American zone, the Nazi party was banned, and its influential or especially active members were made to account for their past records (more than one out of every four adults in this zone were found to be liable under the de-nazification laws).

GERMANS no longer knew what to believe. The incredible crimes which the Nazis had committed were unknown to many of them. They shrank back before the blazing anger and disgust of the invaders who had liberated hordes of crawling, living skeletons from Belsen, Buchenwald and dozens of other concentration camps. Except in their churches, most Germans had no one to whom to turn. The younger generation could no longer believe what their elders told them. School children saw their teachers marched off to be interrogated, even to be imprisoned—for nazism had been strong in the teaching profession. Hundreds of thousands of refugees began to arrive from the old German provinces beyond the Oder. Society seemed to have disintegrated. One foreign correspondent called the Germany of 1945 "a country where men had lost all hope, and women all shame."

WHAT was to be done with the German people, who had welcomed the rule of a gross tyrant and had served him so well that he had nearly conquered Europe? In spite of mingled emotions of guilt, disillusionment and despair, Germans were still shocked when they learned of the plans of their conquerors. The Allies talked of dividing Germany into entirely separate states and giving large slices of German territory to various victor nations. In the meantime they failed to agree on fixing Germany's frontiers. They were determined to extract reparations by dismantling industrial equipment and removing it. They also proposed to limit production by imposing a "Level of Industries Plan," which might well prevent Germany from supporting itself. The victor nations visualized a military occupation of Germany that might last as long as 20 years.

Had the Russians collaborated honestly in the postwar settlement of Germany, there is no knowing how long the country would have been treated as a defeated enemy. But the Russians insisted, in defiance of their allies, on extracting reparations from current production (over and above dismantling) in their zone of occupation—and also in the British zone, which included the Ruhr. They walked out of the four-power Allied Control Council which had been set up in Berlin to frame and implement unified policies for Germany. They fomented the cold war. In particular, they imposed a blockade of Berlin in June 1948 that lasted almost a year.

This situation made the division of Germany more absolute, but it also led the Allies into a reversal of policy toward their former enemy and thus brought some compensations for the people of West Germany. Gradually the western powers began to compete with the Russians for German support in the cold war. As early as September 1946, the American Secretary of State, James F. Byrnes, had said in a speech in Stuttgart that the German people must be given self-government and the chance of earning a decent living. The American and British governments were forced to pour in big subsidies in order to bolster the reeling German economy: in 1947 alone, these came to around $600 million. In August 1947, the "First Level of Industries Plan" was modified; the American and British zones, which earlier that year had merged into one economic unit, were between them allowed to produce up to 10.7 million tons of steel a year, against 5.8 million tons for all of Germany in the earlier plan. The dismantling program was substantially changed: for example, heavy machinery to be dismantled was cut by almost 50 per cent. In 1946 and 1947, the *Länder*—the main administrative units of West Germany, each one being called a *Land*—were allowed to hold free elections and form governments. This marked a significant advance from the purely local administration which was all that had at first been entrusted to the Germans.

IN the spring of 1948 the French agreed to unite their zone of occupation, mainly for economic purposes, with those of the United States and Britain. The three Allied powers next decided to give the whole of West Germany a democratic, federal constitution and its own parliament. The *Länder* parliaments elected a constituent assembly, which sat in Bonn from September 1948 to May 1949, producing a constitution (called the Basic Law) and enabling the first national elections to the *Bundestag*, the more important of the two houses of the federal parliament, to be held in August 1949. West Berlin got its own Senate, which acts as a governing cabinet, and House of Representatives, which must approve all federal laws that apply to the city.

The well-being of the new state has depended to a large extent on the effectiveness of the federal government, and in turn on the new constitution. The constitution has been an almost unqualified success. It has safeguarded basic human and political rights. It has established the independence of the judiciary from the legislature. It has given the vote to all citizens who are 21 and over.

ORGANIZATIONALLY, the constitution provided for a president elected by a federal convention made up of all members of the *Bundestag* and an equal number of members from the *Länder*. The *Bundesrat*, the legislature's other chamber, was to have three to five representatives appointed by each of the *Länder*.

Most importantly, the constitution provided for a chancellor to determine policy, and it gave him a strong and stable position. During his tenure of office, the chancellor could be dismissed only by a "constructive vote of no confidence" by the *Bundestag*, accompanied by a vote in favor of a successor and by a request to the president to dismiss the chancellor. The Weimar Republic had not been so fortunate. Between 1919 and 1933 it had had 20 different governments, and the last chancellor—Hitler—had even been able to bring all democratic rule to an end in 1933 through the exercise of emergency powers. The 1949 constitution avoided these pitfalls.

It did much more. It helped to ensure the kind of steady government which the German people needed so desperately. For more than a decade after 1949, successive governments were headed by Chancellor Konrad Adenauer. The election in 1949 was closely contested, with Adenauer's Christian Democrats and the Social Democrats emerging almost equal in strength and between them winning two thirds of the seats in the *Bundestag*. Adenauer accordingly took into his coalition two smaller parties, the Free Democrats and the German party. In 1957 the Christian Democrats won a clear majority over all other parties combined, but on policy grounds Adenauer continued to take in coalition partners. In 1961, when his own party's vote dropped to 45 per cent, Adenauer again took in the Free Democrats as coalition partners. He retired from the chancellorship in October 1963, but remained chairman of his party until his death in 1967.

All the main political parties since 1949 have been eminently respectable. In the 1920s the Nazi and Communist parties worked to destroy German democracy, and the right-wing German National party certainly did not defend it. Since 1945, apart from the wish to make a fresh start, the West Germans have supported democracy for three reasons: a distrust of Communist Russia, a desire for security, and a wish to be accepted into the western European community and to make real friends for Germany. These arguments may not have been presented very convincingly, but the vast majority of the German people regarded—and regard—them as valid.

Most of all, the German people wanted a breathing spell. Many of them had experienced two world wars, the breakup of the empire, the political uncertainties of the Weimar Republic, the inflation that came to its height in 1923, the mass unemployment of the 1930s and the total collapse of 1945. It is not surprising that so many voted for a moderate, middle-of-the-road chancellor like Adenauer and for the Christian Democratic party.

ADENAUER had a strongly developed political intuition. During his years in office, many Germans laughed over his foibles—his refusal to brook argument from his ministers (or to allow them even to smoke at cabinet meetings), his reliance on the advice of "experts," his devastating use of small-town wit, his dislike of unflattering photographs of himself. Yet Adenauer was a rounded personality. Discrimination, humor and human interests gave Adenauer his fullness of life. They also helped make him a great leader. Winston Churchill once called him "the greatest [statesman] in Germany since Bismarck," but generations to come may put Adenauer first and Bismarck second. For Adenauer set the German people a supreme example of constructive action in politics and common sense in thought.

AFTER World War I a great many Germans embraced "Europeanism" and roamed Europe bearing olive branches and expressions of good will—thereby lulling the victors into an unwarranted sense of security. Two and a half decades later, Adenauer embraced "Europeanism" in a different spirit—because he believed it to be the sole salvation of his people. He made friends with France, knowing that most Germans—above all, German youth—would support this. He built up friendly relations with the United States. He supported the supranational European institutions which came into being, and even some—like the proposed European Defense Community—which did not. His efforts paid off. In return for making real friends and for agreeing to a West German contribution to the North Atlantic Treaty Organization, Adenauer won sovereignty for the Federal Republic through step-by-step agreements. At home his constructive and enterprising—though conservative—economic policies speeded Germany's material recovery.

Adenauer failed, however, to secure any progress toward German reunification. It may be that his foreign policy became too inflexible, for he made no move to exploit the apparent Soviet desire for a relaxation of tensions in Central Europe or to develop better relations with Poland and the other Soviet satellites. Possibly, Adenauer clung too long to office, and it was the growing force of public opinion which eventually forced his retirement from the chancellorship in 1963.

He had concentrated what many critics considered undue power in his own hands, and he had ruled through a devoted chancellery staff rather than through the cabinet and the *Bundestag*. Another complaint against Adenauer was that he built up the central government's power to the detriment of the *Länder*. The original intent had been to achieve just the opposite. Both the French and American governments opposed undue centralization in 1949, and the *Länder* were given the major share of control over the police, full control of education and cultural affairs, and a measure of control over economics, finance and justice.

This made for a more even distribution of power between central and regional governments than Germany had ever enjoyed. But it did not solve all governmental problems. Only a minority of the *Länder*—like Bavaria and the city-states of Hamburg and Bremen—were historic entities with their own traditions; others were artificial creations. Since Adenauer's time, the *Länder* have regained much of the significance they had in the late 1940s and have been effective in implementing federal laws. Should Germany ever be reunified, however, a more centralized system focused on Berlin no doubt will evolve.

STILL another complaint against Adenauer was that he created a "chancellor democracy." Dependence on Adenauer the father figure for important decisions slowed the growth of the spirit of self-reliance and the full participation of the individual in the workings of the democratic state. It reduced the authority of the *Bundestag*. Yet this was not altogether Adenauer's fault. After so many national disasters it was natural for him to concentrate on sound administration. In addition, years of authoritarianism made it hard for Germans all at once to think of themselves as full-fledged, politically active citizens.

The average citizen, indeed, has little contact with his representative in parliament. He does not send his complaints to him. During political campaigns there is no house-to-house canvassing. Politics are regarded as a matter of expertise, not as a method of articulating public opinion. Germans still tend to say, "That's a political matter; it's got nothing to do with me, and what could I do about it anyway?" The Germans may have felt a special need for a father figure after 1945, for they felt utterly cast adrift after the collapse of their world. The force of German public opinion is nonetheless growing. Franz Josef Strauss was forced to resign as defense minister in 1962 after he had brought about the jailing of Rudolf Augstein, publisher of the magazine *Der Spiegel,* for publishing an article on defense matters which Strauss charged had revealed military secrets. Public opinion was responsible for Adenauer's retirement and for the termination of an ugly struggle over the succession to the chancellorship between himself and Vice Chancellor Ludwig Erhard.

ADENAUER was over 87 years old at the time. Yet he remained determined to block Erhard, a man who he believed lacked *Eigenschaften*, or talent, in the political field. Adenauer may have thought that circumstances might bring a better politician to the forefront—just as he himself had emerged in 1949, a party chairman who had taken that job only because he had been sacked from his post of Lord Mayor of Cologne by a shortsighted British official. Adenauer set a high value on his own blend of wisdom and opportunism, a combination illustrated by his original election as party chairman in 1946 at a Christian Democratic conference in Herford. The man who had called the meeting was a Dr. Holzapfel, but Adenauer took the chair with the words, "I presume I am the oldest among those present. If no one objects, I may therefore consider myself president by seniority." In Adenauer's view, Erhard lacked this sort of ability to seize the moment and, in addition, knew too little about foreign affairs.

Apart from public backing, two factors combined to make Erhard chancellor in 1963. He had been the choice of the entire party as vice chancellor and the party preferred him to any conceivable rival. He was, second, widely regarded as the architect of economic revival. As such, he would be a trump card in a Federal election. Rosy-cheeked, genial, with an air of well-being and the aroma of prosperity given off by his eternal cigars, Erhard appeared to be the right man to lead the country in the second stage of its democratic experiment.

He was a different man from Adenauer in other ways as well. He tried to work more closely with his cabinet, to foster better relations with both the Free Democrats and the Social Democrats, and to achieve a more balanced relationship with all of West Germany's allies in the Atlantic Community. But he faced opposition not only from the other two parties but also from within his own party.

Erhard was confronted, as well, with a worsening of relations with France and with internal troubles in the Common Market. De Gaulle was angered by the absence of automatic German support in the Common Market, which always had been available in Adenauer's day, and he sensed a German challenge to his efforts to establish French leadership in western Europe—a challenge due to Erhard's belief in free-trade principles, his desire to promote the "Kennedy Round" of proposed tariff reductions and his disappointment over the exclusion of Britain from the Common Market. Nevertheless, under Erhard's leadership, the Christian Democrats were able to win 47 per cent of the votes in the 1965 Federal election, thus ensuring their continuance in power for another four years. The Social Democrats, however, increased their strength, winning 39 per cent of the vote.

IT is ironic that Erhard, author of the German "economic miracle," ultimately had to resign because of an economic crisis. The recession that began in 1966 proved one more reversal than he could handle. His call for higher taxes and spending cuts alienated the Free Democrats, whose participation in his government had given him a majority in the *Bundestag;* their four cabinet ministers resigned and the parliamentary majority was gone. At the same time, the Chancellor lost the backing of his own party when Adenauer, who had always opposed Erhard, aligned himself with the younger men in the party ranks. Forced to admit failure, Erhard resigned in November.

He was succeeded by Kurt Georg Kiesinger, the Minister-President (governor) of Baden-Württemberg. Kiesinger realized that another coalition with the Free Democrats would provide only a slim and tenuous majority. He therefore became the first CDU Chancellor in history to form a coalition with the rival Social Democrats, who added almost 40 per cent of the *Bundestag* to his 47.6 per cent. Called the "Grand Coalition" because it was made up of the two major parties, this government took office on December 1, 1966.

KIESINGER was largely unknown in West Germany when he became Chancellor. By contrast, his partner in the Grand Coalition, Willy Brandt, the head of the Social Democrats, had earned a worldwide reputation during his nine years as mayor of West Berlin. Other contrasts abounded; Kiesinger was a Catholic from the south of Germany and an ex-Nazi, while Brandt was a northern Protestant and a former Marxist. The suave and elegant Chancellor was known to Germans as "the fox"; his gruff Vice Chancellor was called "the bear." Together they began to give West Germany new strength of purpose both at home and abroad.

In the realm of foreign policy, the Grand Coalition departed radically from the former West German attitude toward the eastern European bloc. Reversing the policy of Adenauer, who had held that reunification of Germany must precede any détente in relations with the East, Kiesinger sought to establish both economic and diplomatic relations with members of the Soviet bloc. At the same time, West Germany began to assert its independence in the NATO community. At home, the Grand Coalition was forced to cope on the one hand with a new right-wing party and on the other with active demonstrations by left-wing dissidents. Moreover, there were rifts within the Coalition itself. Still, the new government met with remarkable success in facing up to its greatest challenge, reviving a flagging economy.

The Free Democrats, the only opposition party since the formation of the Grand Coalition, have survived in the *Bundestag,* where only 5 per cent of the total vote secures representation. They regard themselves as torch-bearers of liberalism but have obtained much of their support from middle-class conservatives. Their outstanding member was Professor Theodor Heuss, Federal President from 1949 to 1959. With his mane of white hair and his courtliness salted with dry Swabian humor, Heuss proved the ideal man to say the right word to the German people at the right time—on national shame at Nazi misdeeds or on national modesty as a means of making friends. But Heuss was aloof from party politics. The Free Democrats found an able new leader in 1960 when Mende was elected party chairman. In 1965, under his direction, the Free Democrats took 9 per cent of the vote.

OTHER splinter parties have come and gone. The Communist party was banned in 1956. The Refugee party lost strength as former members became fully integrated West German citizens. The 1966 state elections marked the emergence of the neo-Nazi National Democratic party, which won 7.9 per cent of votes cast in Hesse and 7.4 per cent in Bavaria. Two years later, in Kiesinger's home *Land,* Baden-Württemberg, the NPD polled nearly 10 per cent. Despite some concern, most analysts agreed that these gains did not indicate any serious drift toward the extreme right by the German electorate.

It is all for the best that there are only three parties which count today in the Federal Republic. The fragmentation of political parties in the Weimar Republic between 1919 and 1933 prevented stable government, encouraged sectional interests and lent support to the fallacy that politics are a matter of combination and manipulation and not the expression of the positive views and wishes of a determined people. During the postwar years, Adenauer produced the kind of stable government which, for Germany's sake, must prevail.

What of the political future of the Federal Republic? The present holds good omens. The new government seems soundly rooted now, and its people seem reasonably contented. It has plenty of healthy features. In spite of perennial jokes about the "federal village" of Bonn, whose only useful building is said to be the railway station, parliamentary government is generally accepted. The press has become more vocal, critical and watchful. A very high percentage of Germans cast their votes in elections. Women have become more emancipated politically—possibly because they now comprise more than a third of the labor force, possibly because the ferment of defeat and the loss of manpower led them to desert the German tradition of *Kinder, Kirche, Küche* (children, church, kitchen). More than 10 per cent of the *Bundestag's* members are women, and a woman, Elisabeth Schwarzhaupt, became Minister of Health in 1961, and has since been replaced by another woman, Käte Strobel.

Wild national ambitions have vanished and have been replaced by a steady desire on the part of most Germans to avoid political experiments, to increase their material well-being and to be good Europeans. Federal and *Länder* governments have applied democratic principles. Best of all, there is a real sense of personal liberty throughout the country.

TO be sure, there are some clouds on the German horizon. While the West German economy seemed as sound as ever in the late 1960s, reunification appeared to be far off and the Soviet Union was still determined to keep Germany divided. The question of Germany's eastern frontier was still not settled. The drive toward European union had been halted, and the members of the Common Market were at odds with one another. But the almost 60 million West Germans have discarded what the historian Karl Adolf Menzel called "this lamentable doctrine that God will not desert his Germans." They have returned to an older creed. A hundred and thirty years ago Goethe wrote, "Let us remain in league with advancing life and test ourselves when opportunity offers." Advancing life, for the West German, means resolution to defend his freedom and to remain loyal to the western alliance.

HEAPED CORPSES at Buchenwald are shown to Germans in 1945. U.S. troops forced nearby inhabitants to inspect such camps at the war's end.

IN ANGUISH, a mother (*right*) seeks news of her son at a center for prisoners released by the Russians in 1955. She learned he was still being held.

Heritage of War and Defeat

Germany was deeply scarred in the Nazi years, and the horrors it inflicted on the rest of the world fill a fearful page in history. Some six million Jews, among whom were numbered some of the greatest of European intellectuals, businessmen and politicians, died amid the terrors of concentration camps like Buchenwald and Belsen. The number of others who also suffered from Nazi persecution is unreckoned. With such a heritage of horror, it is the more miraculous that West Germany today is not only prosperous but stable, led by able men who are dedicated to democratic freedoms.

Wer kennt ihn?
Leutnant
Heinz Krüger
geb. 24.3.1919 in Eberswalde.
Heimatanschrift:
Breslau, Clausewitzstr. 4
Feldpost-Nr. 19812 A
Vermißt seit 14.1.1945
bei Radom, Polen.
Er war Adjutant beim Abt.-Stab
Artillerie der 214. Inf. Div.

A NEW NATION *was founded by constitutional convention in 1949*

STATE'S FATHERS include the cigar-smoking Socialist Carlo Schmid (*above*) who was elected vice president of the *Bundestag*, the lower house in Bonn.

NIGHT SESSION at Bonn (*left*) keeps delegates and office workers late in the converted school building on the Rhine which served as the constitution hall.

SOLEMN DELEGATES listen (*right*) to committee proposals. The constitution provided for a president but gave real power to a federal chancellor.

ABLE POLITICIANS *have led the Federal Republic in the postwar years*

AGING LEADER, Konrad Adenauer *(left)* served as West German Chancellor from 1949 to 1963, when he retired. He remained politically active until his death in 1967.

ASTUTE ECONOMIST, Ludwig Erhard *(above)* succeeded Adenauer as Chancellor and head of the Christian Democrats. Unable to hold support, he resigned in 1966.

COALITION PARTNERS, Chancellor Kurt Kiesinger *(right)* and his Vice Chancellor and Foreign Minister, Willy Brandt, confer during a cabinet meeting. Kiesinger, head of the Christian Democrats, and Brandt, head of the Social Democrats, formed a "Grand Coalition" in 1966, after no single party could muster a clear majority.

IRASCIBLE CHIEFTAIN, Franz Josef Strauss (*above*) leads the Christian Democrats' Bavarian branch. In 1966 he became Finance Minister in the Kiesinger government.

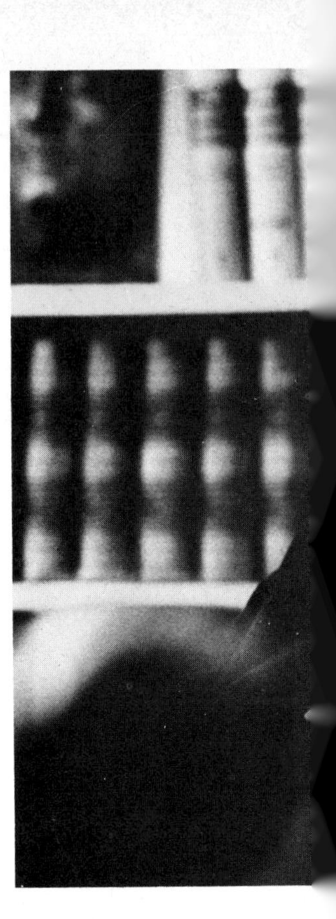

OUTSPOKEN MINISTER, Christian Democrat Gerhard Schröder (*left*) held the foreign office portfolio under both the Adenauer and the Erhard regimes. He became Kiesinger's Minister of Defense in the Grand Coalition.

RIGHT-WING LEADER, Adolf von Thadden (*right*) heads the neo-Nazi National Democratic Party, which emerged after 1966 as a formidable force in local German politics, capturing up to 10 per cent of the vote.

EPUTY CHAIRMAN of the Social Democrats, Herbert Vehner (*above*) served for years as chief party strategist nd became Minister of All-German Affairs in 1966.

MINOR-PARTY BOSS, Erich Mende directs the Free Democrats. When the Grand Coalition was formed in 1966, the small FDP became the only opposition party.

IN ENDLESS FILE, completed Volkswagens roll from the company's Wolfsburg plant. Volkswagen produces more than one million automobiles and trucks every year.

A Prosperity Reborn

"I began to look for the crushed and starving, and desperate and bled-white Germany," a British journalist, Douglas Reed, wrote after World War I. "I never found it. I found a country that had never known war on its own land . . . that had called the war off when the inevitable defeat impended . . . that by this apparent surrender had warded off decisive military defeat . . . a country that . . . was beginning to hope that it had outwitted its foes."

Germany presented a very different picture after World War II. For nearly three years its people faced a desperate shortage of food. In the big towns bread lines sometimes stretched a hundred yards down the streets from the bakeries. Even potatoes became one of the most sought-after commodities traded on the flourishing black market. Townspeople were reduced to a daily ration of 1,100 to 1,300 calories, but even this amount was often not available. "Substitutes" became common: for meat there was dried fish and for butter there was *quark*, a tasteless cottage cheese made from skim milk. On the black market a single cigarette sold for a dollar and a half. A pound of butter might cost $80. The hospitals were filled with people suffering from malnutrition.

The outstanding impression that Germans of those days gave to a foreigner was that they had literally shrunk. Their clothes often hung about them like sacks. They were tired, listless and demoralized. The prevalent prewar type of German—confident, corpulent and possessed of a loud voice and an obvious surplus of energy and arrogance—had almost vanished.

NOWHERE was this change more apparent than in the Ruhr, Germany's industrial heart. The Ruhr—the 2,000-square-mile industrial belt near the Dutch border, running from Duisburg in the west to the other side of Dortmund in the east and containing around eight million inhabitants today—had begun to have economic significance as early as 1830, after the perfection of the blast furnace. At that time, iron ore was being mined farther to the south, in Siegen and the Sauerland. Shallow coal seams around Essen and Mülheim were being exploited, and 100 or more mines—many of them then uneconomic—were in operation. Friedrich Krupp was beginning to cast steel in his works at Essen, and the Rhine and its canals provided a convenient highway for freight traffic, with growing river ports at Duisburg, Düsseldorf and Cologne.

But the immense development of the Ruhr's industrial potential got under way only in the second half of the 19th Century. New methods of mining coal, new processes of steelmaking, the speeding-up of transport and the appearance in the Ruhr of Swedish and French iron ore—these were factors which changed the face of the area and produced what one economist, Gustav Stolper, called "an industrial organization which in its compactness and intensity is unparalleled in the world." By the turn of the century the population of one of the towns, Essen, had multiplied 80 times since 1800. About 200 coal mines were working efficiently, and huge reserves of coal had been proved.

The output of the Ruhr enabled the German war machine to work with precision during World War I. It inspired the French military occupation of the Ruhr in 1923, when the French believed in vain that this act would ensure payment of German reparations. It was a blessing to Hitler when he was struggling to gain power, for some of the Ruhr industrialists helped to subsidize the bankrupt Nazi party. In time, the Ruhr also provided the basis for Hitler's military gambles.

The Ruhr industrialists, moreover, built up cartels on a huge scale in order to fix prices, secure big profits, control markets, achieve strong bargaining positions toward trade unions and keep their companies expanding. The biggest concerns, the Krupp, Flick and Stinnes trusts, built their power on coal and steel, but they also controlled a wide range of other forms of industry. Hitler not only tolerated the cartels, but promised their organizers new empires in countries subsequently overrun by the Nazis during the war.

BUT when Hitler lost the war, the Ruhr suffered more than any other area its size in Germany. Its towns had been terribly battered by Allied bombs. Now much of its industrial plant was dismantled and carted off as reparations. Other plants were forced to remain idle under the Allied "Level of Industry Plan," which restricted industrial output to what was mistakenly imagined to constitute basic needs, so that a teeming and skilled urban population had to remain idle too. Many Ruhr miners traveled dozens of miles into the countryside to trade or beg a bag of potatoes. They waited in uneasy groups along the railway lines to pick up a few lumps of coal. They pulled little gocarts into the woods to gather twigs.

The Ruhr's turning point came only three years after the end of the war, and its history thereafter is symptomatic of the economic recovery of West Germany as a whole. In 1948 a "Ruhr Authority" was formed by the western occupation powers and the Benelux countries (Belgium, the Netherlands and Luxembourg) with the aim of allocating coal and steel for home consumption and for export. Other European countries wanted German coal and steel. In spite of this, there was a tendency to restrict German steel production because of outworn reasons of "security." Then in 1950 the French Foreign Minister, Robert Schuman, produced his plan for a "European Coal and Steel Community." France wanted a steady supply of Ruhr coal and hoped that the internationalization of the Ruhr would prevent the area from becoming a purely German asset, and France made certain that the Schuman Plan operated in its interest when it came into existence. The Germans actually were forced to deliver Ruhr coal to France and to import American coal to make good their own needs. But the Schuman Plan was one of the steps which led to the formation of the six-nation Common Market in 1958. After France, West Germany has been the Market's biggest beneficiary. The Market has stimulated German industry and has pointed up the need for an overhaul of German agriculture. It has also helped to give West Germany greater political influence in Europe.

This influence has been won because the Germans have shown themselves to be disciplined members of the Market and loyal supporters of the recommendations of the Market Commission. The Germans have had to defend the interests of their agriculture against challenges posed by France, but they have been the foremost exponents of lowering tariffs and of freeing trade—originally the primary aims of the Market.

THE growth which has taken place has been spectacular. West Germany's gross national product has more than tripled since 1950. A housing shortage of six million homes has been all but eliminated. West Germany became Europe's biggest maker of motor cars. In 10 years steel production quadrupled, with Germany becoming the world's third largest steel producing nation (after the U.S. and Russia). Virtually new industries like petrochemicals and electronics came into existence. The *Deutschemark*, which replaced the worthless *Reichsmark* at the time of the 1948 currency reform, became one of the most stable currencies in Europe. Twenty years later, gold and foreign exchange reserves totaling almost eight billion dollars had been accumulated by the German Federal Bank.

The dry facts of the "German economic miracle" tell only part of the story. The German citizen was affected in all sorts of ways. Admittedly, he often continued to live in a small utility flat, which had been built in rather too much of a hurry at the time of the grievous housing shortage. Admittedly, he took time to accumulate personal belongings to replace those lost during the war or traded away to the farmers for food before 1948. But he was earning good money, and he became one of the readiest spenders in Europe.

HE ate more and drank more and spent more on clothes and holidays. In the 1960s Germans were eating more meat and butter than they had been in 1950—but much less "basic" bread and potatoes. They were drinking twice as much wine and considerably more beer than they had been in that period. German tourists were spending over one billion dollars outside the country annually. They gave whole tourist areas a strong German flavor—the Italian Riviera from Ventimiglia to Genoa, the Adriatic coast from Trieste to Ancona, the Tyrol, the Dolomites and the Balearic Isles.

Out of this prosperity was born a new generation of intense and single-minded business tycoons. Take one example—that of Max Grundig, West Germany's first postwar electronics millionaire. In the small industrial city of Fürth, near Nuremberg, Grundig has built up an empire founded on radio and television sets and tape recorders. He set up shop in 1946 with only a few dozen workers; in 1965 he was employing 30,000. He is one of the biggest radio manufacturers in Europe, and his

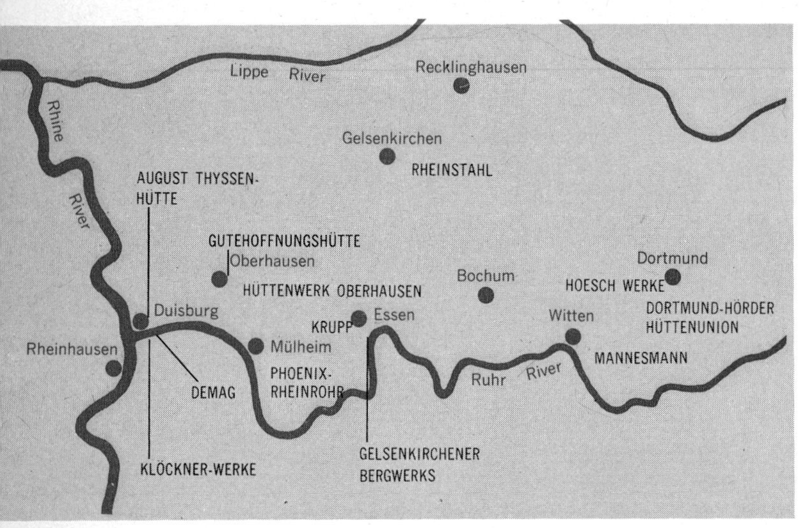

THE MIGHTY RUHR, the industrial heartland which produces the bulk of West Germany's coal and steel, is shown on the map above, with the main plants of the region's 12 largest firms indicated in bold type. South of the river from which the area takes its name, heavy machinery, textiles and chemicals are manufactured.

tape recorders are among the world's biggest sellers.

The West German standard of living today is one of the highest in Europe. The purchasing power of wages exceeds that in any other western European country. Today the German workingman leads a comfortable life and wears a well-filled waistcoat. He eats well, and his food—although German cooking lacks the elegance of French—is wholesome and appetizing. He buys good clothes, and he dresses his wife and children well. He generally has money to spare for television sets, weekend excursions and football matches. And he is not afraid of celebrating occasionally on a grander scale.

West German housing conditions are good, although some homes are still a little cramped. Plumbing is of a higher standard in Germany than anywhere else on the European mainland except Switzerland, Holland and Sweden. Some 70 per cent of the homes have bathing facilities. Standards of town planning are high, and there are no slums of the kind that can be found in any Mediterranean community or even in the North and Midlands of Britain. Municipal authorities have considerable powers and resources for the acquisition of land for building, and they use both without hesitation. The drift to the cities which began in the 1880s goes on, and the population of Düsseldorf, for example—about 500,000 just after the war—rose by 40 per cent in 20 years. Work began in 1957 on a big "satellite town," a housing center for 50,000 people five miles outside Nuremberg, and this way of providing homes has seen increasing usage in more recent years.

Of course there will be more or less urgent housing problems in West Germany for a long time to come. The country's population rose from 44 million to almost 60 million in two decades. This was in part caused by the arrival of some 200,000 refugees a year from East Germany and in part by the surplus of live births over deaths. All things considered, however, the population is not increasing rapidly. The plain fact is that working-class families no longer expect to have five or six children as a matter of course. Improved living conditions have made them more money-conscious, more interested in material welfare, perhaps more selfish—and therefore less anxious to have big families.

HOW is it possible to explain the "German economic miracle," which has produced so much progress and comfort such a short time after the country was bankrupt, overrun with refugees and largely in ruins?

The first explanation is that the Germans have worked desperately hard. The German is industrious by tradition, and after 1945 he had less than ever before to distract him from his work. He left politics to the professional politicians. With his country divided between two power blocs and under enemy occupation, he saw little purpose in worrying about big issues. So the average German concentrated on his job, spurred on by the desire to build up what he had lost.

The economy benefited greatly from American economic aid, which amounted to more than $3.5 billion in all, the bulk of it becoming available after 1948, when it was most needed. Paradoxically, West German industry may have been lucky to have had so many of its factories dismantled and removed as reparations after the war. Germans themselves admit this. Many industries were forced to start from scratch and were therefore modernized much earlier than they would otherwise have been; there is a marked contrast between the modern plants of the Ruhr, for example, and those of the Liège and Charleroi coal and steel areas of Belgium, where much steelmaking equipment needs to be replaced.

As the West German Minister of Economics from 1949 to 1963, Ludwig Erhard naturally deserves much of the credit for the country's economic revival because of his "Free Market Economy" policies. He was chiefly responsible for the jettisoning of the "Ahlen Program" drawn up by the Christian Democrats in 1947, which envisaged the public ownership of the coal and steel industries. Ironically, Adenauer himself had supported this now-forgotten plan. But Erhard was convinced that the Germans, given freedom and incentive to earn, would work harder than ever before. He liberalized the restrictions on imports, lowered tariffs, and arranged tax advantages for business concerns —and introduced his programs with a remarkable flair for timing.

Erhard was one of the architects of currency reform, which brought goods back into the shops and dealt the black market a death blow. He called for sacrifices to maintain a sound currency and was loyally backed in this by the Federal Bank. He boosted exports through carefully planned incentives.

PLENTY of credit also should go to the West German Federation of Trades Unions, which in the national interest has discouraged use of the strike weapon since the war. The unions have preached moderation in wage claims and have combated underground Communist activity in the factories. West Germany's "strikeless" record is remarkable: in a typical year, 1964, only 16,711 working days were lost because of strikes by a labor force of 22 million. This compared with 2.3 million working days lost in Britain (with a labor force of 25 million) and some 23 million lost in the United States (with a force of 75.5 million).

Two other factors in the German recovery are important. One was West Germany's freedom from the burden of defense commitments until 1955, which allowed the economy to progress normally. A second was the fantastic boom in securities prices in the 1950s. Immediately following World War II most common stocks—as a result of war damage, dismantling and postwar unemployment—appeared to be almost valueless. But Germans who were wise or lucky held onto their shares. One speculator, the Bremen timber merchant Hermann Krages, made a huge fortune with stocks he bought "at the bottom"; it has been estimated that he made a profit of about $50 million out of the shares of the Vereinigte Stahlwerke steel combine alone. Such speculative activity has had one positive result: big firms have found it easier to raise new money for expansion.

FINALLY, it is palpably true that a new spirit of hustle and progress has dominated postwar Germany. It is no coincidence that the new class of industrial managers dresses like its American counterpart and works at the same tempo, or that Europe's first supermarket on the American model was set up in Cologne. To U.S. observers, the German businessman's imitation of all things American may not appear very striking, but it is a phenomenon that is noticed by other Europeans. So is German acceptance of the American gospel of unlimited economic opportunity for the ambitious.

Before the war the industrial scene was dominated by the "great" families of the Ruhr: the Thyssens, Haniels, Poensgens and Krupps. It was a group from this industrial elite that supported Hitler and helped finance the Nazi party in 1933 when it was threatened with bankruptcy. The real support began in January of that year when the Cologne banker Kurt von Schröder presided at a meeting of some of the richest industrialists in Germany, at which the decision was made to back Hitler financially. Later a group of magnates, including Gustav Krupp, met with Hitler and Goering and pledged their support—backed by a contribution of three million marks.

With the defeat in 1945, some of the great prewar tycoons lost their power. But others—like the Krupps, Thyssens and Flicks—were successful in re-establishing themselves. Meanwhile, a number of new industrial empires were created—by Max Grundig in Nuremberg, by Josef Neckermann's mail-order business in Frankfurt, by the nylon-stocking manufacturer Hans Thierfelder and by Rudolf Oetker, who has built his family pudding-powder business into a composite empire which includes breweries, shipyards, hotels, insurance and banking organizations, paper mills and chemical plants.

A sense of hustle has also come to the farms. Under the "Green Plan," small farm holdings are steadily being consolidated into compact and more efficient units, and government subsidies have been given to speed the program. A hundred and ten thousand East German farmers have been settled on the soil. Their industriousness is proverbial. "We shall set a new pace for the sluggards," one of them told a reporter. "We can manage if need be on a handful of potatoes, and still work hard."

The winegrowers are doing well, too, in spite of an aging labor force and the threat of price undercutting by French and Italian wines, which are generally cheaper. In 1964 there was a record grape harvest of almost 185 million gallons, and while production has remained high, the quality, delicacy and bouquets of German white wines are being maintained with a painstaking care that has been passed down for hundreds of years. The fragrant Moselles, the fuller, richer wines of the Rheingau and Palatinate, the pure Franconians with their greenish glitter—these have a charm and individuality which can be matched by few French white wines.

Industrial workers have their wage demands—but in what democracy is this otherwise? Farmers have their grumbles—they would not be farmers if they had none. The rich industrialists have their failings—they have remained divorced from the rest of society and physically isolated in their luxurious villas. One of them once boasted of having modeled his front gate on the doors of Alcatraz! As a group the businessmen reveal a tendency to rebuild the cartels, and this has led to price-rigging, discrimination against small traders and the weakening of the middle class. But thanks to laws passed by the Federal Republic, cartels are unlikely to recapture the position they held in the 1930s, when AEG and Siemens controlled four fifths of the electrical industry, IG Farben half of the chemical industry, and UFA all German film production and marketing.

Throughout the early 1960s the "German economic miracle" continued to prove itself afresh—exports mounted and there were wage increases of 9 per cent in one 12-month period, while the cost of living rose only about 2 per cent. In general, West Germans seemed contented as well as prosperous. They had full employment. At the time it was said that if a recession should come, it would probably hold more political dangers for West Germany than economic ones. Indeed, when the postwar economic boom slackened in 1966, and West Germany experienced its first recession in 20 years, the repercussions were a major contributing factor to the resignation of Ludwig Erhard as Chancellor. One of the main challenges of the coalition government that replaced him was to end the recession and revitalize the German economy. By means of budget cuts, deficit spending and the levying of new taxes, the government of Chancellor Kurt Kiesinger managed to meet the crisis. Within a year the German economy had begun a new upsurge.

"GIVE us ten years," Chancellor Adenauer had said in 1949, "and we shall be over the first hill." The Germans are well over that first hill. But there is still a tendency to regard well-being as more important than real democratic freedom, and democratic freedom itself as no more than a useful by-product of joining up with the West.

Shift ended, a homeward-bound workman walks his bicycle near the smoking chimneys of one of the Ruhr's numerous steel mills.

Rugged Sinews of an Industrial Titan

Transformed somewhat later than most other western European nations by the Industrial Revolution, tireless Germany quickly became an industrial titan. Today, despite the catastrophic destruction of World War II, it is again a giant. The reconstructed steel mills and blast furnaces of the Ruhr flicker in the night. Factories and research centers pour forth a continuing tide of products. To the muscular economy of Germany, the war might never have been.

THE HOUSE OF KRUPP *is a giant in industry*

GALA DINNER in the Krupp mansion in Essen celebrates the company's 150th anniversary. Seven years later, in 1968, the family firm became a publicly owned business.

LAST SCION to head the company, the late Alfried Krupp (*opposite*), stands by a portrait of his great-grandfather, who produced munitions for the 1870 war with France.

Night lights from the steel mills of Rheinhausen, part of the rebuilt Krupp works, cast a spectral glow across the Rhine River. This

and Krupp's three other steel plants together produce about 10 per cent of West Germany's total crude steel and pig iron every year.

PROSPERITY *is reflected in the availability of a wide variety of goods, services and amenities*

MASS HOUSING rises around Munich. A burgeoning population has spurred work on a series of "satellite towns," combining apartment houses and one-family homes.

TELEVISION TOWER glows above Stuttgart (*right*). Containing a restaurant, it transmits the signals of Stuttgart's station and those of one of the two national channels.

ARTFUL TENTS display gardening equipment and outdoor furniture at a Hamburg exhibition. Backyard living, American style, came to West Germany during the 1960s.

LUMINOUS BUILDING of Daimler-Benz in Stuttgart shines above a display of its automobiles. Besides making cars, Daimler-Benz is Germany's leading truck manufacturer.

NEW TECHNIQUES *stimulate and sustain the industrial boom*

SHINING SPOOLS of rayon await shipment in this automated Dormagen mill. The West German textile industry was a pioneer in plant automation in postwar Europe.

RESEARCH REACTOR in Munich, housed in a thin-skinned aluminum dome *(opposite)*, produces radioisotopes. West Germany has more than 25 such reactors.

VW

STURDY VOLKSWAGENS *reach world markets*

ODD CARGO, a young elephant en route overseas rides through Bangkok in a Volkswagen pickup. Volkswagen products lead the German export list.

ABLE MANAGER, Heinz Nordhoff was responsible for VW's spectacular postwar success. He led the company from 1948 until his death in 1968.

HARD-WON SUCCESS *is enjoyed by the Albert Blocks, a refugee family which has prospered in the postwar years*

CHEERY BLOCKS gather at breakfast. A chauffeur after the family escaped from eastern Europe in 1945, Block earns about $212 monthly in a factory near Bonn. He also repairs furnaces

BLOCKS' HOUSE, erected in 1959, was built with a $6,000 government loan which he has since repaid. Block commutes back and forth to work in his small, German-produced Ford.

BOYS' RETREAT is a bedroom on the upper floor of the Block home. Both boys have about completed the German equivalent of high school and both plan to go on to universities

At Christmas 1964, a horse-drawn cart jolts through East Berlin. East Germany possesses few trucks and cars. The one in the background

probably belongs to a westerner visiting during the holiday.

5

In the Shadow of the Soviet

THE Iron Curtain which divides Germany is formidable, but it used to be far from impassable. For many years East Germans poured daily into West Berlin—their obvious escape route to freedom—or across the borders of the Federal Republic. Nearly three million persons fled East Germany between 1949 and August 1961, when the Berlin Wall went up; since then the flow of escapees has become a trickle. Only about 100 East Germans a month have made it into West Germany since 1961.

Figures are mundane and have no human content. That is why it is too easily forgotten today just what being a refugee means. Fairly typical is the story of the Janke family who left their home in a town in Saxony; it tells more than any amount of statistics can.

The Jankes owned a small textile factory. For a long time the factory had been unimportant enough to escape the attention of the government and the fate of all key industrial plants in East Germany—conversion into a *Volkseigener*

Betrieb, or People's Own Firm. But the day came when the father was told he would have to carry out a state contract that was utterly beyond his capacity. The father knew what this meant. Failure to fulfill the contract would bring an "invitation" to accept state participation in financing, management and ownership. The pattern of these "invitations" is not always identical; but the odds were that the state would offer a 40 per cent financial stake, accept a 40 per cent share in ownership and install its own manager.

This would, of course, be only a first stage. Next would come the expropriation of the owner and his relegation to the position of an employee in the firm he had once owned. The father decided not to wait any longer. He told his family to pack—but to include in their luggage only immediate necessities. Each member of the family was to carry only a small suitcase, and they were to split up for the journey to East Berlin. In this case the mother traveled with her younger son, ostensibly on a sightseeing trip. The elder boy went up with a party of students. The father came last of all. He too went by train.

THE four members of the Janke family met in East Berlin and went in pairs to the metropolitan railway. This line runs from East into West Berlin, and out again to Potsdam in East Germany. The family took tickets to Potsdam; but they got off at a West Berlin station. Soon they were lodged at a West Berlin transit camp. (This escape route was cut in 1961, when the East Germans made it impossible to ride into West Berlin without going through a strict check in East Berlin.)

The Jankes lost everything—home, factory, belongings, even friends and older members of the family who stayed behind. They were aware that their relatives and friends would be under Communist suspicion from then on: all those who had known the Jankes would be subjected to protracted interrogation by the police, their mail would be strictly censored and they would probably never be granted a travel permit to any place outside the East German borders.

The Jankes spent some weeks in the West Berlin transit camp of West Marienfelde. Then they were sent for another 12 weeks to Giessen, one of the two big refugee camps in the Federal Republic (the other is Uelzen). Only then was a temporary home located and jobs found for the father and the elder son. Only then could the family begin its new life, in freedom.

Not even the well-guarded bulk of the Berlin Wall was able to halt efforts to escape from Communist Germany in the months after it was built. In incredible feats of bravery, East Germans fled to freedom by ramming through the Wall in trucks, by tunneling under it and, on occasion, by literally leaping over it.

TO be sure, movement between the two German states has been two-way. Up to 1961 some 30,000 people moved each year from West to East, some of them former members of the banned Communist party. Perhaps one in every four of those who went back was an East German who had not found life in the Federal Republic as golden as anticipated, or who had left behind in East Germany a mother, a fiancée, even a wife and children who had been subjected to pressure by the East German security services.

East Germany is a police state. There are about two and a half times as many policemen —*Volkspolizei,* or People's Police—per capita as there are in the United States. The State Security Service, an organization used both for counterespionage and for internal security, numbers about 17,000 full-time agents. The police have unlimited powers of arrest; a prisoner can be interrogated indefinitely without charges being brought against him. He can be imprisoned for life for "political crimes," the chief of which is opposing the Communist regime's policies.

Living in a police state includes a nominal freedom to vote. In East Germany it is virtually obligatory to vote for one of the parties licensed by the regime, to support the all-party

Blockparteien, or National Front, and to subscribe wholeheartedly to government policies. The 400 seats in the *Volkskammer,* or East German parliament, are parceled out by the *Volksrat,* or People's Council, of the National Front. A handsome majority of the seats go to candidates of the 1.7 million-member *Sozialistische Einheitspartei Deutschlands,* or Socialist Unity Party of Germany—formed by the forced union of the Communist and Social Democratic parties in 1946—and to Communist-controlled mass organizations such as the Confederation of Free German Trade Unions, the Free German Youth and the Democratic Women's League of Germany. A fixed number of seats also go to the Christian, Liberal, National and Peasants' Democratic parties, which are little more than puppet organizations. The Social Democratic party is banned except in East Berlin.

Rigged as it is, the *Volkskammer* is only an organization for rubber-stamping government decrees. All vital decisions are made by the Central Council of the Socialist Unity (Communist) party, of which the veteran Communist Walter Ulbricht is First Secretary. These decisions may be initiated and modified by the Council of State, which was set up in 1960—but its chairman also is Walter Ulbricht. As nearly as possible, the system is modeled on that of the Soviet Union. The root of the power is the party high command. And the party is controlled by Ulbricht.

FEW dictators have been more absolute than Ulbricht—although his power is at the whim of the Kremlin. He has a genius for organization, an immense capacity for work and an undeviating loyalty to Moscow. Born in Leipzig in 1893, Ulbricht joined the Social Democratic party in 1912 and became a member of the German Communist party in 1919, the year it was founded. In 1933 he fled from the Nazis; he later became a Soviet citizen and was with the Red Army during the war. More significantly, he became the Soviet choice as leader of the German Communist party in exile.

Ulbricht returned to Germany with the Red Army in 1945 and watched his fellow Germans surrender. He filled the new concentration camps which took the place of the Nazi ones. He placed key government and party members in a "Red Ghetto," surrounded by barbed wire and protected by police in order to insure their isolation. He implemented every Soviet directive: the blockade of Berlin and the continuing pressure on the city, the nationalization of virtually all East German industry and agriculture, the sharper separation of the two German states from one another, the buildup of the East German armed forces and the integration of East Germany in the economic system of the Communist bloc.

WHAT is Ulbricht's East German state really like? First of all, it is not the bankrupt, backward place which overenthusiastic West German propagandists make it out to be. East Germany, like the Federal Republic, ranks among the world's top 10 industrial producers. On a per capita basis, the industrial production of East Germany is about three fourths of that of West Germany.

And there have been special reasons for the lagging of East German production behind that of West Germany. The Russians, after bleeding the country white following the war, have continued to take reparations out of current production, although these nominally ended in 1954. One reparation still being taken is uranium, which is mined in Saxony by a labor force estimated at 50,000, then shipped to the Soviet Union and almost certainly paid for at cut prices.

The second reason for slower East German economic expansion is that three fourths of the country's exports go to Communist countries. East German industry has been largely cut off from its old markets in West Germany. Finally, the East German economy is organically weak. It is far too dependent on lignite, and there is very little coal.

Yet, in spite of these disadvantages, and in spite of a severe labor shortage caused by workers fleeing to the West, there has been considerable economic progress in East Germany. As a satellite, East Germany is supposed to gear its production to the needs of the Soviet bloc. In fact, since 1960 East Germany has been the leading trade partner of the Soviet Union and its main supplier of chemicals and equipment. Output of machinery, in which East Germany leads the other Soviet satellites, has doubled since 1952. A steel industry was created out of next to nothing. Production of petrochemicals has benefited from the new oil pipeline from the Ukraine, which was built with Soviet aid. The pipeline is believed to be bringing almost five million tons of crude oil into the country annually.

THE emphasis of East German economic planning is on the development of heavy industry, for this is the best way of exploiting German techniques and know-how and a labor force which is still highly skilled in comparison with those of most other Communist countries. The concentration on heavy industry has meant neglect of consumer goods. Like other Iron Curtain countries, East Germany has deliberately been assigned a shortage economy.

Clothes and shoes are seldom of good quality. Household goods are permanently in short supply—it is common experience to see something in a shop window and to find that this article was for display and is not stocked. A phrase which is used even by officialdom and the Communist press is "the thousand small things that are lacking." The fancy goods which make such a brave show at the Leipzig Trade Fairs—Meissen porcelain, Thuringian glassware, Saxon toys and leatherwork—are simply not available to German shoppers. They are earmarked for export.

This is one of the reasons why everyday life in the East German Republic is so gray and drab—even though the standard of living is about the highest in the Communist bloc. There has been too little new building—only one new home is built in East Germany for every 10 in the Federal Republic. The roads are in poor condition, and even the surface of the *Autobahnen* (superhighways) is badly worn—although there is an average of only 14 private cars for every thousand East Germans, against 100 for every thousand West Germans. There is a severe shortage of doctors. Over all hangs an air of listlessness. A subway station, trolley stop or village square is no longer a place where people stop to chatter and laugh. Life is terribly earnest.

Beyond the convinced Communists, who, West German intelligence organizations agree, do not make up more than 10 to 15 per cent of the population, there are undeniably some beneficiaries of the Ulbricht regime. One group which undoubtedly benefits is the Free German Youth, to which half of the population between 14 and 26 belongs. They have a virtual monopoly of sports facilities for the young, and they get cheap holidays in hostels at the best beaches on the Baltic, on the lakes of Mecklenburg and in the hills of Thuringia. Every worker's child is guaranteed a university education. All this is very reminiscent of the way in which the Nazis set out to capture youth. Members of the Communist-controlled trade unions, many of whom are not convinced Communists at all, are given similar advantages. The Ulbricht regime has made considerable efforts to win over members of the intelligentsia, partly by financial inducements and partly by allowing them freedom as long as they do not openly question Communist dogma.

ONE such member of the intelligentsia is a man whom we may call Herr Blank. He is the editor of a periodical which is Communist-licensed but which is given a fair degree of freedom to follow its own interests. Herr Blank does not have to propagate Communist ideas openly; he only has to avoid criticizing them. He can travel abroad occasionally, a rare privilege for an East German. In private he is ready to admit that some official policies may have been too vigorously implemented. He concedes, for example, that the collectivization of the land may have been hurried through without farmers having been given time to appreciate the "benefits" of losing their land; and the imprisonment of political opponents of the regime was an "unfortunate necessity." But he honestly believes that his part of Germany is better off than the Federal Republic. The Soviet Union's insistence on winning the cold war in the economic field, he says, will bring a steadily rising standard of living in all the countries of the Communist bloc.

Herr Blank admits that life is not superficially as attractive in East Germany as it is in the Federal Republic. But he insists that the true standard of comparison is between life in East Germany today and life there 15 years ago. Today there is enough to eat. No man is molested if he goes about his business and shows no sympathy for western "imperialism" and "militarism." The average citizen is better off than he used to be, and he should be content with his lot.

OPTIMISTS like this man are certainly a small minority in East Germany. There is an ever-present undertone of fear throughout the country—and for obvious reasons. Political opposition to the regime is a crime. Refusal to "volunteer" for the People's Police or the armed forces can bring reprisals against a whole family. Huge numbers of East Germans spend every weekend in forced labor on roads and buildings. Young people are regimented and ideologically trained in the Free German Youth and in the more than 600,000-strong Association for Sport and Technology.

Farmers have been forced to surrender their land and join cooperatives. Christian churches have been subjected to intermittent persecution: children are enticed away from confirmation classes by being persuaded to take part in semi-pagan "youth dedication" ceremonies; church baptism is now paralleled by a "state naming" ceremony; and church marriage is officially frowned on.

Nor has de-Stalinization restored as much freedom in East Germany as in other eastern European countries. Unlike other members of the Soviet bloc, East Germany remains a total satellite of the Soviet Union and has not developed a "national communism" of its own. In East Germany, de-Stalinization brought only material benefits. Khrushchev's departure merely increased the sense of insecurity of the Ulbricht regime and reminded it of the need to maintain an iron control over the minds of its subjects. Ulbricht sees the Sino-Soviet quarrel simply as a source of weakness for his Soviet benefactors, and not as an opportunity to win a measure of independence for his people.

WHAT of the future of the 17 million East Germans? Material conditions are strained; prosperity still seems many years away. Food rationing was abolished in 1958, but partially reintroduced in 1961. There will continue to be shortages—some seasonal, but others planned. Politically, East Germany is likely to grow further apart from West Germany, which does not recognize its regime or have official relations with it (although intra-German trade continues).

East Germans are desperately unhappy about the division of Germany, a division whose abnormality was re-emphasized by the building of the Wall through Berlin. Before 1961, many were talking of "our republic" and showing signs of developing a new type of national consciousness. Some were proud of East German achievements, gained in spite of Soviet reparations. But, despite the relaxation of tensions in eastern Europe, the Wall emphasized their isolation, increased the undertone of fear in the state and gave East Germans the feeling that the division of Germany was permanent.

Meanwhile, the state is omnipresent as well as omnipotent, making itself known in the banners and giant placards on public buildings and city squares, in the marching squads of soldiers and armed factory guards, in the uniformity of the Communist-controlled press, even in the ostentatiously worn Communist badges of merit which have been awarded to some 1.6 million citizens. East Germany is indeed worthy of the Kremlin's praise.

AN ECHO OF NAZISM is sounded by goosestepping guards at a war memorial in East Berlin. This practice has completely disappeared in the West.

YOUNG CHARGES, Dresden kindergarteners perambulate through the city. Teachers are required to begin ideological training with this age group.

The State's Constricting Hand

East Germany was perhaps the richest of the spoils that fell into Russia's hands after World War II. While much of the area's farmland is poor and its mineral resources are meager, the industrial skills of its citizens have made it a major bulwark of the Soviet empire. For that reason, and because of its proximity to the West and the continuing possibility that it may rebel against its overlords, East Germany is closely watched by the Kremlin. With one policeman for every 160 citizens, plus an unknown number of undercover agents, the constricting hand of the state is everywhere.

THE PARTY'S MEN *exercise a tight control*

DAPPER COMMUNIST, party secretary Walter Ulbricht, boss of East Germany since 1945, addresses a group at Karl Marx University, formerly the University of Leipzig.

SOVIET SUPERVISION is emphasized (*right*) by a 1965 visit of Russian Premier Aleksei Kosygin (*third from left in reviewing stand*) and other top Soviet officials.

MODEST PLEASURES *are on occasion made available to the citizens of the organized state*

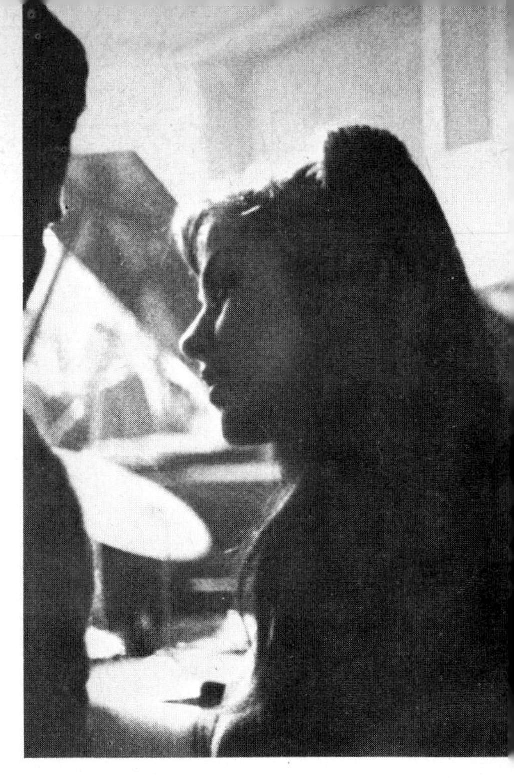

STUDENT COMBO, a group from Dresden's Tech-nical University (*above*) offers American-styl[e] jazz. Despite government opposition, both jaz[z] and western dances are popular in East German[y]

GOVERNMENT SPA at Bad Schandau (*left*), a place renowned for its mineral waters, offers inexpensive vacations to party functionaries and workers, as do other resorts owned by the state.

ELEGANT DINERS take supper (*below*) in the expensive Astoria Hotel in Leipzig, which is usually reserved for officials. The mural depicts supposed U.S. atrocities during the Korean War.

TRADE FAIR held in Leipzig attracts visitors (*right*) to a display of computer components. East German machine tools and electronic devices are of high quality, but consumer goods are shoddy.

EMPHASIS ON YOUTH *marks the people's state*

A CAMPUS PAIR at the Dresden Technical University meet after class. East Germany spends twice as much per capita on education as Bonn.

RED TUMBLERS, members of the Communist Free German Youth (*opposite*) form a pyramid at a sports festival held yearly in the Leipzig stadium.

FLEDGLING MEMBERS of the Communist party, six- to 14-year-old Pioneers perform joint maneuvers with a giant rubber ball in the Leipzig stadium.

ROBUST MARCHERS of the Free German Youth *(opposite)* stride through the stadium. Half of all East Germans aged 14 to 26 belong to this group.

KRONE

RUINED SPIRE of the old Kaiser Wilhelm Memorial Church, flanked by a new chapel and bell tower (*right*), stands in West Berlin. East Berlin is beyond the ruin.

6

A Capital Without a Country

WHEN the well-known British novelist Graham Greene shortly after World War II wrote the movie script for *The Third Man*, a stark, moody melodrama set in postwar Vienna, he could well have chosen Berlin instead for the setting. The story that he told in the film—of hunger, deprivation and the black market, of snatched joys and the nightmare unrealities of life in an occupied and divided city—was equally true of both Vienna and Berlin at the time. Vienna returned to normality not long after; Berlin today still has an unreal and frightening feeling to it.

The strangeness of the city is not so immediately obvious as it was just after the war. Some poverty still exists in West Berlin, but it hides itself. The black market has gone; so has the smuggling between East and West Berlin which was long a profitable business. The pursuit of pleasure has become a more hectic

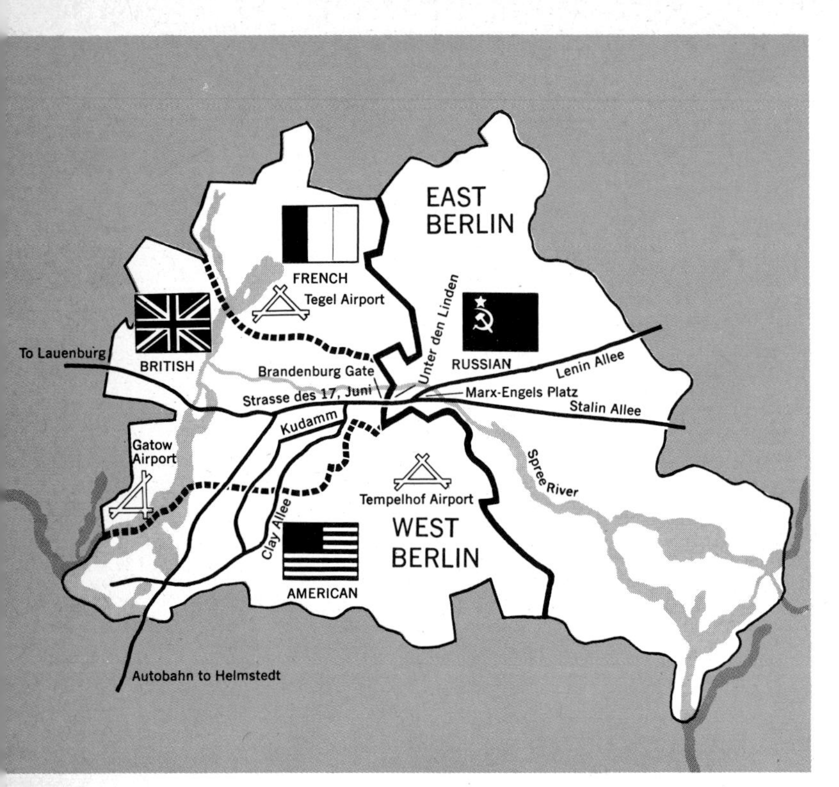

DIVIDED CITY, Berlin lies 105 miles east of West Germany. The border between Soviet East Berlin and the western sectors was set by the 1945 Potsdam Conference.

affair, carried on against a background of eternal uncertainty in free West Berlin and of continuing fear in East Berlin.

Berlin is a city of spy and intelligence services, and kidnappings by Communist agents still occur at times. Citizens—both disreputable and respected alike—still suddenly disappear. It is impossible to telephone directly from West to East Berlin, even across 100 yards of ground; the wires were disconnected years ago. It is impossible to buy an East German newspaper in West Berlin, or the reverse. It is illegal to use the money of one part of the city in the other, although there is a small unofficial trade in both currencies.

Even before the erection of the Berlin Wall in 1961, cooperation between the two halves of the city was capricious and arbitrary. If a traffic accident took place close to the boundary and the injured persons lay on West Berlin territory, an East Berlin doctor often found himself prevented from helping. Criminals used to move —as they did in *The Third Man*—between the eastern and western sectors. Neither side wanted to shelter "ordinary" criminals, and the two sectors occasionally used to work together to catch them. Then the police of the two Berlins met on the boundary, discussing the matter with their feet on the proper sides of the line.

Political lines were drawn even at the grave. Just outside the borders of West Berlin in East Germany proper, there is a cemetery in which a great many West Berliners of earlier generations are buried. Sometimes the East German authorities issued permits which allowed West Berliners to visit the cemetery; sometimes they refused to do so. When they refused, the West Berliner—barred from laying a wreath on his father's grave—could only look at it, across a few yards of East German territory.

West Berlin's very existence, as a free city surrounded by an unfree East German state, is circumscribed by unreality. There is a 105-mile gap to the nearest point of West German territory, at Helmstedt. Traffic between Berlin and the West is restricted to four roads, three air corridors, four railway lines and one waterway for the barges which carry about 30 per cent of West Berlin's imports and exports. It was the Russians' arbitrary closing of the surface accesses to the West for 11 months in 1948-1949 that constituted the so-called Berlin Blockade, a move which the western powers finally thwarted by successfully supplying West Berlin by air.

POLITICALLY, Berlin is divided into four sectors, of which three, the American, British and French, make up West Berlin. The Soviet sector serves also as the capital of the East German Republic. Both East and West Berlin have their own city administrations and assemblies. But while those in East Berlin are purely municipal, the West Berlin bodies have sovereign rights, and these rights are only limited, by mutual agreement and for special reasons, by the three western powers that maintain garrisons in the city. These "retained rights" of the western powers, governing security, emergencies and certain other matters, are in no way resented by the West Berliners. For they underline the legal grounds for the continuing presence of western garrisons, as authorized under the London Protocol, an agreement which was signed by the major Allied powers in 1944.

UP to the summer of 1961, there was a fair degree of free movement between West and East Berlin, with occasional bouts of arbitrary interference by the East German People's Police. The building of the Wall radically altered the situation. Concrete, five to seven feet high, topped by yards of barbed wire, it was a massive reminder of the division of the city. The reasons for its erection were obvious. An average of 320 refugees a day used to stream into West Berlin; not long before the Wall's erection, the total had increased to some 1,500 a day. Clearly, so large an exodus benefited neither the East German economy nor the long-term desire of the Soviet Union to make the division of Germany final.

The Wall immediately slowed the flight of refugees to a trickle. The *Volkspolizei* became increasingly alert, and increasingly trigger-free. Tunnels were dug, canals were swum in the dark of night, and people jumped to freedom from the third and fourth stories of houses along the boundary line. Today, only a scant handful of East Germans escape daily into West Berlin.

Travel into East Berlin itself also came under harassment. For a long time West Germans were permitted to enter only if the East Germans decided that they were on "official" business. From 1964 to 1966, however, the East Germans allowed West Berliners to cross the border on certain occasions to visit relatives. Military traffic between West and East Berlin, and between West Berlin and West Germany, has also been intermittently harried, as has travel of West German officials across East Germany. In 1961, while East German party boss Walter Ulbricht was shouting his agreement with the Soviet demand that West Berlin be made a "free," demilitarized city, shorn of its western garrisons, President Kennedy recalled General Lucius Clay, the U.S. Military Governor during the Berlin Blockade, to act as his special representative in Berlin. For a time, the United States also brought up tanks to the sector boundary, a move countered by one of the rare appearances of Soviet tanks at the border since the East German revolt of 1953.

Inevitably, two rather different human types are growing up on the two sides of the Berlin Wall. The West Berliner has big-city wit, sharpness of mind and self-sufficiency. He is proud that he is *waschecht,* or dyed-in-the-wool, and that he has *Schnauze,* a word literally meaning "snout" but implying the sharp mind and ready answer for which Berliners are known. He is marvelously uninhibited, being ready on any occasion to talk about his views of God, his own sexual habits, his hopes or the uncertainties of life. He is a hedonist, and his immense zest for living combines a coarse, sensual streak with courage, gaiety and common sense. Among all the Germans he is the friendliest, the roughest, the most natural and the most human.

LIFE is conducted in a minor key in East Berlin. Only at the Christmas Market and similar times is there any sign of the old vigor and jollity which used to be so prevalent. On official occasions, such as May Day and the anniversary of the Soviet Union's October Revolution, East Berliners have a marvelous knack for simply not appearing. Every second person on the crowded streets seems to be a Saxon; the rest are workers who have been brought in from Mecklenburg, Thuringia or Brandenburg. An East Berlin restaurant is always a sorry place, where sad-looking waiters serve bad meals at a snail's pace and go through the motions of refusing a tip. At night, when half the population of West Berlin seems to be strolling on the Kurfürstendamm, the ill-lit streets of East Berlin are deserted. Houses stand dark and silent.

West Berlin has many distinctive features, East Berlin few. The West Berliners love light and air; wherever you see a flat roof, there you will be sure to find a little garden, an awning, a table and chairs, a small essay in living. West Berliners love dogs—they cherish mongrels. The city's dog population is vast and much in evidence.

The West Berliners love movement and the countryside. The lakes lying in a chain from the Tegelersee in the northwest to the Wannsee in the south, all of them within the boundaries of greater Berlin, are crowded in spring and summer. The people are avid for news, and West Berlin is one of the few German cities with a fair range of evening and Sunday newspapers. Berliners like pretty women, and they like just about every kind of entertainment. West Berlin has an opera house, a score of theaters and more than 100 movie houses. It has its own eight-team football (soccer) league and endless facilities for swimming, indoor roller skating, tennis, gymnastics and boxing. It even has that rare thing in Germany, a first-class golf course.

The night life of West Berlin is notable for its variety, robustness and peculiarities. West Berlin has the biggest night entertainment center in central Europe—the Resi Bar, with its pneumatic tubes for sending messages between tables, its 250 table telephones and its water shows with 10,000 jets and a hundred thousand colored lamps. West Berlin also has a number of less reputable nightclubs, with men dressed as waitresses and female impersonators in the floor shows. This propensity for the postures of perversion is left over from the 1920s, when Berlin became the Babylon of Europe, an unsavory hatchery of prostitution and homosexuality, and even of sadism practiced in so-called "massage saloons."

BUT West Berlin today also has plenty of small, intimate, "normal" boîtes of the continental pattern, with good music, soft lights and a dash of saucy but healthy entertainment. West Berlin for that matter has one of the best political cabarets in Europe, *Die Stachelschweine* (The Porcupines). Its shows consist of a dozen or so short sketches, each with a political and mainly topical flavor. Biting satire is the keynote of each sketch, but a note of honest sentiment or genuine pathos can be discreetly introduced. German political cabaret has one supreme virtue: it does not just amuse, it makes people think.

Indeed, West Berlin has much to commend it: the aromatic pines of its rough, forested parkland called the Grunewald, the splendors of its Dahlem Museum, the breadth of its boulevards, the inexpensiveness and variety of its restaurants, the vigor of its artists' colonies and the elegance of some of its women.

East Berlin has much less, and it has nothing of West Berlin's unique mixture of freshness and exoticism. Except for a noteworthy municipal opera, a good symphony orchestra and the little-known "People's Lakes" in its southeast corner, its main features are outsize monuments—the boulevard-like Stalinallee with its execrably ornamented façades, the huge Red Army war memorial in Treptower Park, the Ulbricht Sports Stadium, the Brandenburg Gate with its renovated topknot of the Quadriga of Victory.

THE efforts of the East German authorities to transform their part of Berlin into a real capital city began in earnest only after the wall was erected. New buildings and smart shops line the Unter den Linden (under the linden trees), once Berlin's proudest boulevard. Similarly, the old "government street" of the Wilhelmstrasse has acquired a number of new embassy buildings. The former Lustgarten, renamed Marx-Engels Platz, has become East Berlin's Red Square. An "international" airport has been built at Schönefeld, and a "government ghetto" for ministers and party bosses has been established on the northern outskirts of the city, where the Communist elite can sleep safely and in comfort—far removed from the surly population which rose against them in June 1953.

The 1953 revolt, like the 1948 blockade, was an epic example of the Berliners' sturdy independence of mind. What began as a harmless demonstration of factory and building workers on the Stalinallee on June 16 developed into the risings which took place all over East Germany on the day following. The building workers downed tools and marched to the East German government headquarters to demonstrate against the raising of work norms—the increasing of output minimums while rates of pay remained the same. On the next day similar demonstrations occurred in almost every East German town of consequence.

IN East Berlin huge crowds assembled, tore down Soviet flags and marched through the streets chanting slogans of freedom and of independence from Communist dictatorship. They were dispersed only by the arrival of Soviet tanks, and were finally repressed only by the imposition of martial law and the execution of some of their leaders. Hundreds of East Germans who demonstrated on June 16 and the next few days were imprisoned. Many of them were kept in jail for years and some even died there.

The East Berlin rising was the most dramatic of all the crises which Berlin has passed through since 1945. These crises have brought real leaders to the fore in West Berlin. Ernst Reuter and Willy Brandt have been the most outstanding. Reuter, a onetime Communist who became a Social Democrat and an outspoken anti-Nazi, was elected Oberbürgermeister of the whole of Berlin in 1947, but was never seated due to Russian objections. He was then re-elected Mayor of West Berlin alone, and held office from 1948 to his death in 1953. His rakish beret, his glutinous yet stirring voice and his unquenchable courage in fighting for West Berlin's freedom made him the city's best-loved figure after the war. Brandt succeeded to the post of mayor only in 1957, but he had held other appointments in the city from 1949 onwards. He maintained the traditions established by Reuter—of united all-party government, close cooperation with the western powers and resolution in maintaining the morale and independence of this "island of democracy" behind the Iron Curtain.

East Berlin's Intourist restaurants, its Red Army soldiers in their baggy trousers and tunics, its red banners and monster poster-pictures of party immortals remind the observer that Berlin has always seemed to stand on the frontier of Asia. Between Berlin and the Ural Mountains, 1,800 miles to the east in Russia, there is only the endless plain, whose size is expressive of Asia's infinitude. The beginning of what is now Berlin was a village called Kölln, built by Slavs around 400 A.D. Kölln's first five centuries were not recorded by history, and no one knows how a neighboring village which grew up across the Spree River came to be called "Das Berlin." The Germans arrived in Berlin under Albrecht the Bear in 1134. Berlin received its charter as a free town in 1230, and in the next century began to merge with Kölln. For a time Berlin was the property of the Luxembourg dynasty. Then it was bought by the House of Hohenzollern, but rose in unsuccessful revolt against its ruler. The Bear Rampant of Albrecht, Berlin's coat-of-arms, became a bear on all fours, carrying the Eagle of Brandenburg on its back—the Hohenzollern eagle.

BERLIN was a community of relatively little consequence until it became the capital of the Electorate of Brandenburg at the end of the 15th Century. In the 1680s pavements were laid and a law was passed prohibiting pigs from running in the streets. The population jumped from 6,000 to 20,000 in a few years, and about this time the first linden tree was planted on the future Unter den Linden. From 1701 until 1871 Berlin's history was identified with the soldierly, sober, Protestant Kingdom of Prussia, of which it was the capital. One publican hung this sign over his front door:

A Prussian heart, a glass of beer,
What more need be expected here?

Berlin had 172,000 inhabitants in 1800, and it had 400,000 by 1840. In 1905 there were two million, and six years later more than 3.5 million. This sensational growth was the result partly of the concentration of government and garrisons (Berlin became the capital of the newly founded German nation in 1871), partly of a tremendous industrial upsurge and partly of the extension of its boundaries to include the suburbs. The city's industries included machinery, electrical equipment, motor cars, optics, chemicals, clothing and books.

World War II reduced Berlin from eminence to desolation. The Allies dropped more than 70,000 tons of bombs on the city and flattened 60 per cent of its houses. In 1945 the Red Army seized four fifths of the city's industrial equipment and three fourths of its food stocks. For three years Berlin shared the dismal economic experience of the rest of Germany, and the 1948 currency reform brought no immediate relief. By then the four-power government of Germany had broken down, and in June 1948 the Berlin Blockade began.

THE blockade lasted nearly one year. The miracle of the airlift was its salvaging of the city's freedom. It could not do much to help the city's economy. In 1950 West Berlin exported goods worth $278 million; imports cost more than $575 million. By 1952 the value of exports had approximately doubled, but the bill for imports was more than $700 million. Year by year industrial production rose, too, and gradually the deficit was whittled down. But there is little chance of it being eliminated entirely.

West Berlin has lost the former German government office buildings (now in East Berlin); it no longer functions as a communications and trade center, and it has no agricultural hinterland. Its weird geographical position makes all the more remarkable the economic progress that has been achieved. To be sure, this progress has necessarily been limited. Each year the Federal Republic subsidizes West Berlin to the tune of more than $600 million. However hard Berliners work they cannot pay their way—even with present full employment.

But the Federal Republic is not just keeping a city alive. It is maintaining an invaluable listening post behind the Iron Curtain. It is giving East Germans a last, desperately difficult avenue of escape and the sense of a symbol of freedom. One English writer, James Morris, sees only "ignominy, defiance, futility and opportunism" in the harried life of West Berlin. But to millions of East Germans, Berlin means two very different things—a link with their German heritage, and a hope, however misty, for the future.

West Berlin experienced, at close range and with all the anguish of impotence, the East German rising of 1953. After the Red Army trampled down Hungarian patriots in 1956 the city waited apprehensively for a fresh crisis. With a blend of courage and fatalism—tinged with irritation—it faced the threat of November 1958, when Khrushchev demanded the military and political neutralization of West Berlin. It watched with horror the raising of the Berlin Wall in 1961.

But the Berliners remain wonderfully alert and alive. They proved this by the spontaneous demonstrations of enthusiasm with which they greeted President John F. Kennedy of the United States in 1963 and Queen Elizabeth of Britain in 1965—demonstrations which contrasted sharply with the dreary set-piece shows arranged for visiting Soviet statesmen by East German authorities.

BERLIN, once the proud, arrogant, florid capital of a united German Reich, has ceased to exist as such. The divided city is symptomatic of a divided Germany, with one half ground down by dictatorship and the other confronting a hazardous future. The Berliners themselves, with their stout hearts and their instinct for self-mockery, survive—making up such slogans as "Pass this on! Laughter shared means resistance redoubled!" But the two million or so who live in the western sectors can make no greater contribution to current German history than the resolute maintenance of this outpost behind the Iron Curtain.

SOLID BARRIER, the Berlin Wall cleaves through the heart of the city, emphasizing the division of Germany. Built in 1961, this part has since been thickened.

Courage of a Once-Gay City

Long after Paris and London had become great cities, Berlin remained an outpost, a provincial capital outside the main currents of history. Yet when the city emerged from obscurity, it gave promise of flourishing as brilliantly as any. Before World War I, the Unter den Linden rattled with fine broughams. The Kaiser's court blazed with resplendent uniforms; the Berlin operas resounded to the brightest of tunes.

It was all too brief a time. Today kaisers and ancient linden trees have disappeared and Berlin's music is muted. Although it is once again an outpost, the city in its finest hour demonstrates its greatest qualities: courage and resolution.

94

FUTILE REVOLT, *begun by striking workers, swept through East Berlin on a tide of hope in June 1953, only to be crushed within a day by Soviet armed might*

UNARMED HEROES, East Germans try to fight Russian T-34 tanks with stones (*opposite*). Some 300 tanks and 25,000 troops were required to overcome the rioters.

ENTRAPPED POLICE drop their uniforms in token of surrender. Russian troops were called into action when the crowds overpowered the ineffectual People's Police.

PRESS OF PEOPLE shouting "Freedom! Freedom!" (*below*) halt Russian tanks before government buildings. About 100,000 East Berliners took part in the rebellion.

POSTWAR LEADER, Ernst Reuter, who was West Berlin's mayor from 1948 until his death in 1953, described the city as "an island of democracy in a Red sea."

DEDICATED *to their city, West*

DEFIANT CRY, "Berlin remains free" (*left*) rears high above Willy Brandt, mayor from 1957 to 1966, during a 1959 rally called to demonstrate resistance to Russia.

Berliners of all levels are engaged in a continuing struggle for their freedom

PEERING ACROSS THE WALL in 1964, West Berliners attempt to catch a glimpse of friends or relatives in East Berlin. East Berliners are forbidden to wave back. From 1964 to 1966 East Germany allowed visits by West Berliners on certain holidays; since then, visits have been granted to only a few thousand "distress cases" a year.

On the rustic terrace of the Waldburg Restaurant in Remagen, beer-drinking picnickers dine overlooking the Rhine. Nearby lies the

Remagen bridge over which U.S. forces thrust into Germany.

7

The Peaceable Small Man

THE inhabitants of nations like the United States and Britain are not, on the whole, disposed to argue with the popular images of themselves. Both Uncle Sam and John Bull are easily recognizable and long accepted national types. The leanness of one, the corpulence of the other have been underscored by caricaturists both at home and abroad for years. Not so the popular image of the German. At least among most foreigners, the German has almost always been regarded as an earnest, sturdy and somewhat bullheaded fellow largely without humor. But to a great many Germans, this image has been in error. They have thought of themselves quite differently.

For many centuries, indeed, there has existed in Germany a cartoon figure with whom a large number of Germans have either consciously or unconsciously identified themselves. This is the "German Michel," a thin male figure of indeterminate age, wearing a sort of woolen nightcap on his head, with matchstick legs protruding from shrunken trousers and with an eternally harassed expression on his pinched face. Michel is any man's fool, with an aptitude for being pushed around, a wry comprehension that this is always likely to happen to him and a whimsical humor left at the end of it all. This patient, decent, inept fellow is certainly a long way removed from the popular conceptions of the typical German.

AND yet the German Michel is not purely imaginary. The picture of the average German as a brutal and arrogant bully has never been particularly accurate. The standard German did knuckle under far too much in the past to his superiors. He was at the end of a chain of cuffs and kicks. His mistake—perhaps even crime—was to allow himself to be pushed around. He was the "small man," and he is only today beginning to learn to assert himself. His failure to do so earlier was an intrinsic part of the German tragedy.

About as typical a "small man" as can be found in the West Germany of today is a 45-year-old Berliner whom we may call Kurt Weser. Kurt, a brawny youngster, was taken out of school at the age of 14 and followed the line of least resistance by joining the Hitler Youth, carrying out his semicompulsory *Arbeitsdienst*, or labor service, for the Nazi party and marching to war in 1939, outwardly resolute but inwardly quite undesirous of heroic exploits. "What else could I do?" he asks today. "I just had to take orders. We all did."

Only a month before war broke out, Kurt had again taken the line of least resistance by marrying. To marry young is all very well, but neither the 18-year-old Kurt nor his 17-year-old bride had any settled occupation. On the other hand they were promised a bounty by the Nazi state for each child they produced. Their easy assumption of the correctness of the Nazi population policy may be gauged from the fact that they produced three daughters in three years.

Kurt fought all over Europe and rose to the giddy rank of corporal, and his luck held until 1944. Then he was badly wounded in one leg. But he was, in a sense, lucky once more, for he was captured by the Americans and was sent back, with only a slight limp, to his home in Berlin soon after the war's end. His regiment ended the war fighting the Russians outside Berlin. Some of his comrades came home from Soviet prison camps five years later. Many of them never came home at all.

There were few jobs to be found in 1945 Berlin. Kurt eventually managed to find a place in a pool of truck drivers employed by the British army. From there he moved to employment as driver for a foreign journalist, whom he served with almost feudal loyalty for four years. But the journalist left, and Kurt, now distinctly lame but perfectly cheerful about it, took a job with a trucking firm. He has held it ever since.

It is a tough job. Trucking firms work their long-distance drivers as hard as they dare. They

A GERMAN SYMBOL

Mournful Michel, who is to German cartoonists what Uncle Sam is to American, exhibits an air of bewilderment when confronted with large issues. In the cartoons at left printed by the magazine *Simplicissimus* during the 1965 elections, he examines the rival candidates, then is agonizingly incapable of making up his mind when casting his ballot.

pay bonuses—on the side, for these are forbidden by law—to drivers who can complete an 800-mile round trip, delivering one load and bringing back another, in a day less than the expected span of time. A truck driver operating from Berlin must pass through two East German checkpoints every time he drives to and from West Germany—where virtually all of his firm's business is done. A driver will sleep in his truck when weary, then drive on again and try desperately hard to get back early to the family he sees so little.

How far removed is the existence of this sort of "small man" from West Germany's long-lasting economic boom! Yet Kurt Weser is the sort of man who does not grumble, who cultivates the admirable philosophy of always counting his blessings. He is prepared to find satisfaction in little things, and he is honestly grateful for the lack of constraint which West Germany and West Berlin enjoy today, and which he never experienced under the Third Reich.

Kurt is very much aware of the dangers of Communism and thankful for the presence of western garrisons in Berlin. "The Russians cheat," he says. "They cheat over the stuff I take in and out of Berlin in my truck, trying to make out it's contraband. They keep me waiting for hours at a checkpoint. They cheat over everything—over politics too."

KURT WESER is not unlike the German Michel, though he does not have Michel's helplessness and self-consciousness. There have been times in the past when German "small men" like Kurt have become objectionable to their fellow men—but only when they have been acting under precise orders. At other times—and when not being ordered about—they have been perfectly peaceable. Today they are being given a unique chance of learning to assert themselves.

Yet the evolution of the "small man" toward active and constructive citizenship is no easy or automatic process. Like the German Michel, Kurt has always assumed that he need not be expected to have views on anything outside his own walk of life, least of all on politics. "Which of the political parties do I vote for? Why, for the Social Democrats, I guess," he commented not long ago. "They are supposed to be the workingman's party. But politics mean nothing to me." Questions put to Kurt on any current issues are likely to elicit the same sort of response: "I don't mix myself up in things like that."

Kurt claims that he has too little time to inform himself. He reads little except the newspapers which happen to be in roadside cafés along the routes his truck must travel. Often enough he is too tired to read even these, and fatigue limits the amount of recreation which he can find time for. A glass of beer in a local bar, a Sunday stroll in one of the Berlin parks, an occasional football match or a visit to a bowling alley—these are simple pleasures indeed. Kurt's main relaxation, in fact, is riding his *Moped* (a bicycle with a tiny auxiliary engine). This is the most that a man earning $120 a month can afford.

THE German view of Michel has credited the "small man" with a humorous quirk. At least he has a healthy sense of fun. All through the Rhineland, starting on the 11th hour of the 11th day of the 11th month (November) and reaching a peak the week before Ash Wednesday, *Karneval* time is celebrated with immense gusto, with dancing and carousing into the early hours of the morning, with masked balls (any or practically no costume permitted) and parades through the streets. There is a tradition at *Karneval* time that a kiss may be offered to anyone, or planted anywhere, and that the fun need not stop at a single kiss. An unmistakable earthiness invades whole sections of the community, though there may not be the state of unbridled license which critics (and some admirers) of *Karneval* maintain there is. The event really reflects the German love of dressing up and of being ordered to laugh.

Berlin has a carnival season which is a pale imitation of the Rhineland revels. Stuttgart does somewhat better, while Bavaria, led by Munich, celebrates *Fasching* at the same time of year with greater emphasis on private parties and with a considerably saucier atmosphere.

Kurt certainly approves of *Karneval*, for it takes his thoughts off such gloomy problems as the division of his country, the life that some of his friends have to lead in East Germany and the possibility of war. Indeed, war occupies a surprisingly large portion of Kurt's thoughts, and his feelings about fighting are strong. "For God's sake, no more wars" is a phrase often on his lips. He does not say this just because he was once dressed up in uniform, ordered about and invited to become cannon fodder by a brilliantly gifted madman. For Kurt, as for other Germans, war is synonymous with defeat, degradation and despair. And he cannot see how any other war would have any better result.

THIS may seem surprising to people outside Germany who have heard of the Prussian military tradition. To many people throughout the world, the military tradition which the Prussians imposed on Germany after 1871 was not only awesome; it seemed to pervade the entire country, demanding loyalty and respect from every German citizen. Indeed, the superbly efficient German army which had accepted this tradition was a state within a state, and the members of its Officers' Corps swore a personal oath to the Kaiser. All members of the army were tried only by their own military courts, even for civil offenses. Up to 1918 it even was an "offense" for any officer to fail to punish a civilian who had, in his view, affronted him. Officers swaggered, and Colonel Edward House, whom President Woodrow Wilson sent to Germany as his personal emissary just before World War I, found the atmosphere one of "militarism run stark mad." This was the atmosphere in which the German Michel lived in the old days. It was he who suffered most of all from Prussian militarism.

The Prussian military tradition went on to dominate the 100,000-man *Reichswehr* of the Weimar Republic and Hitler's armies, both of which retained iron discipline and remained isolated from the community. The German soldier expected rough treatment in both world wars; he usually got it.

SOMETHING like a national revulsion against militarism in any form has swept postwar Germany. This has been due only partly to the teaching of the victors, who said that there should be "no more wars, and above all no more German armies to start them." In 1919 the Germans had eagerly accepted the myth that their armies had not been defeated. In 1945 they could not make the same mistake; the invading Allied armies were clear testimony to the collapse of Hitler's *Wehrmacht*.

The Germans learned their lesson almost too well. Some of their former enemies were convinced that when the Germans were invited to take up arms again in 1955 as junior partners in the western alliance, the old traditions would be reasserted. It was argued that a German army, even within NATO, would soon try to dominate the nations of western Europe. And this German army within NATO was being formed in order to balance the East German troops whom the Russians had shown no hesitation in organizing. Would these two German armies not join together in time and once again menace the peace of Europe?

But the revulsion against armies and war had gone much deeper in West Germany than was supposed. There was no movement in favor of rearmament. Instead there was a strong campaign against it under the slogan of *Ohne mich* —"Leave me out of it." The trade unions, the Social Democratic party and prominent clergymen of the Evangelical Church all opposed rearmament. So did German women, who had lost husbands and sons. West German youth showed a passive disinterest.

Kurt Weser's views on all this are as simple as those of the German Michel. Sometimes he may grumble about the tough treatment in 1945 of German soldiers by the victorious western armies. Sometimes he may express a vague dread of a nuclear war. Sometimes he may ask why more has not been done to secure world disarmament. But Soviet policies are sufficiently disturbing for him to welcome the presence of western armies on German soil and the existence of NATO (with West Germany a full-fledged member). His loyalty to the West seems at the moment beyond question.

One external factor has helped Michel to accept West German rearmament. Under Soviet direction the East Germans began raising the paramilitary *Bereitschaften* in 1948. The force numbered around 50,000 in 1950 and already had light tanks and artillery. By 1951 it included five fully mechanized divisions, modeled on those of the Red Army. In 1956 it came out into the open as the People's Army, and in 1962 conscription was introduced. The force numbers about 200,000 men organized into several strategically based commands and six fully trained divisions. Earlier, the East German Air Force had been given Russian Yak fighters. The People's Army is also backed by paramilitary police forces and such civilian groups as the Association for Sport and Technology, whose members are trained in the use of rifles and machine guns.

YET West German rearmament was not finally agreed upon until 1955—and it would be ridiculous to regard the earlier organization of a small frontier police force as a kind of substitute army. Even in January 1959 the Federal Republic had only 186,000 men in its armed forces. By the late 1960s it had almost 460,000 men under arms. These included an army of 12 fully trained divisions and a total air force strength of nearly 100,000 men. These armed forces have been progressively and conscientiously organized in accordance with the terms of the Federal Republic's contribution to the NATO defense system. They will be used only in defense of their country against armed aggression. This is why it is absurd to level the charge of militarism against the West Germans, as the countries of the Communist bloc have been doing.

There is another reason why the German Michel now offers no real objections to the creation of a new Germany army: It is a new kind of army in German history. Its drill has been cut to a minimum. Goose-stepping, unnecessary heel-stamping and excessive saluting have been abolished. Soldiers can now wear civilian clothes when off duty. When asked what he disliked about the old army, Kurt Weser's reply was *"Kommiss,"* or soldiering; the word connotes discipline for discipline's sake, at the disposal and for the benefit of the military martinet. The new *Bundeswehr,* or West German Army, may even suffer from a slight lack of discipline, or at least some of its younger members say it does. But it is discreetly efficient and wonderfully unobtrusive.

West Germany has never undertaken to produce nuclear weapons of its own, but has wanted the NATO command to have the use of nuclear arms so that West Germany would have a voice in their disposal. Therefore, West Germans welcomed the 1963 American and British proposals to create a multilateral nuclear force in which the Federal Republic would participate. More recently, they have balked at signing a nuclear nonproliferation treaty, feeling that this would leave them overly dependent on United States policy, in which they have no say. In general, they want a larger voice in the over-all direction of the western alliance. But their old dreams of military conquest and glory are dead.

THOUGHTS such as these may be a little deep for Kurt Weser, the German Michel. The worried little man with the woolen nightcap may be too preoccupied with the normal business of living. He may still consider that these problems are not for the likes of him. The very thought that he should concern himself about them may fill him with apprehension. "I have my job," Kurt Weser says, "and my family too. I've got troubles of my own." Then, as an afterthought: "But if the western powers are going to keep the peace in Europe, I'm their man."

The Rigorous Pursuit of Fun and Frolic

"A wine barrel that is not tapped," wrote a 15th Century churchman in defense of Germany's uninhibited pre-Lenten customs, "will surely burst." Most disciplined of soldiers, most industrious of citizens, Germans pursue fun with a thoroughness and intensity unrivaled anywhere else in the world. After months of careful planning by festival committees, the untrammeled gaiety of the beery feasts of Cologne, Munich and other cities bursts forth precisely on schedule; like clockwork the wild revelry ceases, and sober, disciplined Germany returns hardheadedly to work.

CAPPED COMIC, winner of first prize for funny speeches at Cologne's *Karneval* chats after his victory. A pre-Lenten outburst, *Karneval* monopolizes the city for three full days every spring.

LADY REVELERS whoop it up (*above*) in a sprawling festive tent at the Munich *Oktoberfest*. This sudsy autumnal party has been an annual event in the city since 1810.

KARNEVAL GAIETY brings waggishly costumed paraders (*left*) into the streets of downtown Cologne. Each of these elaborate festivals takes almost six months to plan.

VIGOROUS ENDEAVORS *in the open air retain their appeal for*

virile devotees of all manner of sports

ALPINE AERIALIST, Siegwart Bach negotiates a cable strung across the Austrian-German border. He made the trip in less time than it often takes on the ground.

BAVARIAN BALLOONISTS rise slowly (*left*) above Augsburg in the annual distance championship. Ballooning has been an organized sport in Germany since 1900.

BB 365

DEFENSE FORCES *of Germany are tied into the western alliance*

MODERN TANKS roll through Olden- ourg in 1962 to mark the entry of the German 11th Panzer Grenadier Divi- sion into NATO. The new army now contains 12 combat-ready divisions.

GROUND CREWS ready U.S.-designed starfighters for takeoff *(opposite)* at Nörvenich airport. Germany contrib- utes its air force of almost 100,000 men to the NATO air-defense system.

MIXED CREW, officers from Italy, Germany and Greece sail aboard a U.S. destroyer to demonstrate the feasibility of operating NATO vessels with crews of different nationalities.

At a West Berlin rally organized by anti-Nazi youth groups to protest an outbreak of anti-Semitism, young Germans demonstrate

indignantly as policemen (left) stand by to maintain order.

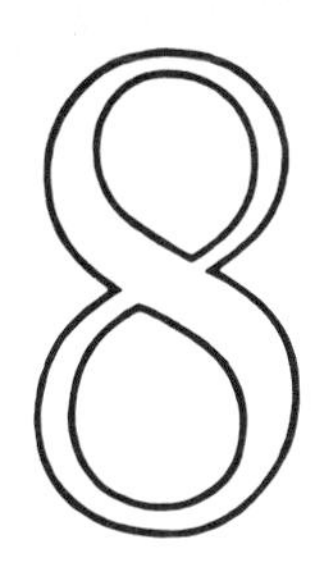

An Undercurrent of Uncertainty

THE chief complaint that West Germans have about life in their own country today is that it is humdrum. Of course it is for the most part a secure and profitable life. The steady economic expansion in the Federal Republic makes it likely that any young man who wants to get ahead will do so. There are plenty of good jobs, with good pay and favorable prospects. Despite these reassuring signs, however, there exists an undercurrent of uncertainty which is built out of all sorts of complexes—guilt, fear and a dread of the past.

There is an old saying that the ordinary mortal works in order to live, while the German lives in order to work. Today, certainly, the West Germans have learned also to spend their money, and when the question was asked in a recent public-opinion survey, "What would you like to have changed in your life?" one of the most frequent answers was, "Eat less."

Superficially, no doubt, there is much that is humdrum about life in West Germany—

and, in a different way, in East Germany as well. The art of conversation has withered, although this has happened in other European countries too. A contemporary German writer, Paul Schallück, has observed, "We do not even have any time to reflect," and he blames this lack on "the thrice-accursed economic miracle, which has robbed a whole generation of the joy of living." The art of debate is moribund—partly due to the sad example of the *Bundestag*, where almost all speeches are prepared in advance and merely read aloud, and partly to the general lack of enthusiasm for new political ideas. Question time after a public lecture in any West German town can be a somber experience: a certain amount of interest is evidenced, but the questions are elementary and offered hesitantly, bolstered with somewhat lame rhetoric.

The art of private entertainment is practiced far less than before the war (although the money for it is there), and a curious reserve is detectable on the part of audiences at public entertainments, even in the night clubs of Hamburg and Düsseldorf, where the most basic strip-tease routine awakens hardly a flicker of interest in the faces of free-spending but indifferent burghers. Young West Germans, to be sure, head off from home in large numbers to see something of the world. But young East Germans are not allowed to travel except to party and "peace" conferences in Iron Curtain countries. Some of the refugees who arrived in West Germany before the erection of the Berlin Wall were, strictly speaking, not refugees at all; they came over partly out of a hope of adventure, but far more in order to earn a good living. Now this is no longer the case.

THE undercurrent of uneasiness in Germany today can be traced largely to the fact that while a great many Germans would like to forget the past, most are unable to do so. To them the past means the uncertainty, the fear and the shame of the Nazi era. And that uncertainty, fear and shame still intrude relentlessly into their comfortable present.

An obvious case of this came to a head in 1960, when the Federal Minister for Refugees, Theodor Oberländer, came under heavy fire. Before the war he had been a leading exponent of German expansion into Russia and German exploitation of Russia's economic potential and living space, and while serving on the eastern front in World War II he had allegedly taken part in atrocities against civilians. The agitation against Oberländer came at the outset from the Communists, who have been waging a massive campaign to try to show that a Nazi revival is sweeping the Federal Republic—with encouragement from Bonn—and who were therefore interested not so much in Oberländer himself as in discrediting West German democracy. The Communist agitation touched off a wave of feeling against Oberländer on the part of decent German and western European democrats. The minister had to resign, even though he had served his government for seven years. He had to resign because he was a cabinet member strongly suspected of war crimes. Later investigation failed to turn up any conclusive evidence of his guilt, but in any event it was an unsettling affair.

THEN there was the case of Richard Baer, arrested in December 1960 after a dozen years of routine service as forester for the current Prince von Bismarck. The last commandant of the Auschwitz concentration camp, Baer had been living under an assumed name for 15 years. There was the case of Franz Schlegelberger, awarded a pension of $700 a month in 1959 in Schleswig-Holstein. Seventeen years earlier he had proposed the deportation or sterilization of all German Jews, adding the suggestion that their formal "consent" should first be elicited. Schlegelberger at the time had been acting Minister of Justice. He was involved in other crimes: he had known, for instance, all about the organized murder of mental defectives and had done nothing to stop it. After the war he was jailed, then released and, in effect, exonerated when the full pension of $700 was subsequently granted to him. When news of the pension spread, there was a popular outcry against him, and his pension rights were canceled (later they were partially restored). Schlegelberger's punishment was mild enough; still, it serves as another example of the difficulty of escaping the past.

CASES like those of Oberländer, Baer and Schlegelberger—and there have been a great many like them—are inexorable reminders of the past. Reminders of this kind are deeply disturbing. For they seem to throw established society into question. Why was a man like Oberländer made a minister when his past was such an open book? The answer—that he was a good administrator at a time when there were few trained men available for the job, and that he helped to keep a section of the refugee vote on the side of the government—is hardly satisfying. True, former Nazis constitute only a tiny minority in the West German government, and most of them have no important influence. But how can a man like Baer survive, leading so ordinary a life? And Schlegelberger's case can be repeated many times over; there are hundreds of ex-Nazis drawing fat pensions, while thousands of victims of nazism have had to fight for the barest restitution.

One should not be too quick to blame the federal government for this state of affairs. Major war criminals were freed after the war by the victorious Allies, and minor offenders came before German courts which were acting under procedures laid down by the Allies. It is next to impossible to prosecute half a nation (seven million Germans were party members, and many thousands of others were active Nazi sympathizers); and it took the federal government a long time to realize that a considerable number of ex-Nazis had managed to escape the consequences of their support of the Hitler regime. In 1958, a central service was established at Ludwigsburg for the investigation and prosecution of Nazi criminals. After that more than a thousand arrests were made and many notorious murderers and sadists were jailed to await trial. The statute of limitations on such crimes was to have expired in 1965, but despite considerable public opposition the *Bundestag* voted in March of that year to extend the statute to 1969. Also in 1965 a Frankfurt court sentenced 16 former S.S. men and a barracks overseer to terms ranging from three years and three months to life imprisonment for the mass murder of prisoners at Auschwitz.

It is significant that when Adolf Eichmann, the former S.S. officer responsible for the murder of millions of Jews, was captured by Israeli agents in 1960, not a word was said in his favor in West Germany; indeed, his trial and execution accelerated a national soul-searching and did much to bring home to the Germans the full horror of what the Nazis had done.

THE average German citizen at least deserves understanding in his predicament of perpetual confrontation with the past. The Nazi era left a state of material chaos behind it, but the mental confusion that was also left was far worse. It is possible to solve problems of supply and transport, even to reorganize a badly shattered economy. It is not so easy to put new ideas into men's minds. Oberländer, Baer, the war criminals, the S.S. men, the maniacs and murderers—here is a Roman frieze which the average German citizen must contemplate repeatedly, and with much bewilderment. It is difficult for him to evaluate the evidence from the past which is still being thrown up in what should today be a settled, forward-looking and contented country. It is equally difficult for him to assess the psychological problems which are inevitably involved.

The reason for this difficulty is that elderly and middle-aged Germans still suffer today from a guilt complex. Even if they opposed Hitler, these people are acutely conscious of their failure to prevent him from wrecking Germany—and Europe. If they did not oppose him, they are likely to find any excuse: they did not know how "serious" it all was, they thought that the Nazi regime would become more liberal in time, they had never heard of the concentration camps, they were helpless to stop Hitler anyway and, finally, they were let down by the western powers who recognized the Nazi regime and thereby strengthened it—and who failed to take seriously the existing resistance to Hitler within Germany.

There is probably as much unhappiness of mind among the millions of Germans who failed to oppose Hitler as among the millions who actively supported him. Many of the latter will admit today how mistaken they were. But at least their mistake sprang from positive thinking. And many of them still seek to justify themselves. In February 1961 a former S.S. general, Erich von dem Bach-Zelewski, was able to stand up in front of the court trying him and say, "I was until the end Hitler's man, and I still am convinced of his innocence."

GRAVE difficulties exist for German parents who are called on to answer their children's questions about the country's past. A great many parents undoubtedly avoid doing so. Many young Germans declare, "It's no good asking father about what happened under the Nazis. He just says the subject is too complicated to discuss." How can a father hope to be a real mentor to his children when he has to admit, at the very least, that he saw Jews being forced to wear the yellow Star of David, being cold-shouldered and bullied, and being furtively removed to unknown destinations—and that he did nothing?

This frequent if not invariable hiatus in family life has not yet been filled by the teaching profession. A great many schoolmasters were among the most fanatical Nazis. There is nothing surprising about this. One need only recall the typical schoolmaster in the film of Erich Maria Remarque's novel *All Quiet on the Western Front*. He persuaded the 20-year-old hero, who was on leave from the trenches in World War I, to tell 14- and 15-year-old boys about the glories of war. He was enthusiastic; the hero from the Western Front was not.

Present-day German schoolmasters may well find it difficult to try to teach the lessons that arise from the Nazi past. Teachers must have a clear, settled and acceptable interpretation of history to transmit to their pupils. Such an interpretation still does not exist everywhere in Germany. Under the constitution, *Länder* governments were granted exclusive control of education, and despite prodding from the Allied authorities they were slow to tackle the business of teaching a dispassionate, fair account of contemporary history.

A textbook being used as late as 1961 in Heidelberg high schools, for example, reported that "the deeper reasons for World War II are to be found in the tensions caused by the 1919 Versailles Peace Treaty." It did not mention Hitler's "reasons" for marching into Poland. The book contained a short paragraph describing Hitler's racial policies and the "killings of millions of Jews," but had no description of the Nuremberg Laws which laid down rules for the Nazis to follow in purifying the "Nordic race."

Better history books are being written today. A tardy but earnest effort is being made to bring the story of the persecutions of the Jews into its true perspective—a task whose importance is indisputable, since it is the Germans themselves who will suffer most from feelings of guilt until the full story has been told.

BESIDES having to weed out fanatical ex-Nazis and correct faulty textbooks, the teaching profession has had many other problems. New textbooks have had to be produced since 1945 (in that year one teacher, with a class of 141 boys and girls, had a single textbook—one he had borrowed). New teachers have had to be trained, for the mass dismissals of ex-Nazis after World War II left a severe shortage. Thus in 1945 the average age of teachers in the United States zone was 52, and half of these were over 60 years old. New schools have had to be built, for classes were fearfully overcrowded (the average class size after the war was 65) and a great many schools were being run on double or triple sessions.

There has been steady progress in solving problems of this nature, but other problems remain. The Roman Catholic Church demands denominational schools with Catholic-trained teachers for Roman Catholic children, and this has led to keen controversy in some parts of Germany. Generally speaking, predominantly Roman Catholic areas provide separate denominational schools for both Catholics and Protestants, while predominantly Protestant regions have "mixed" schools. There is still a body of strong right-wing feeling among university professors, and also among the university *Alte Herren,* or alumni. It is the graduates who have been chiefly responsible for the reintroduction of *Mensur,* or student fencing, which is designed to secure "scars of honor" on cheek and chin. There are plenty of teachers who have come from the lost territories east of the Oder, and they in turn have their own interpretations of history and geography. The schools are still suffering from the poverty of intellectual life under the Nazis. Education in West Germany is going through an adjustment, and this can hardly be a speedy process.

IN time, no doubt, the schools will be playing their part to the full in the regeneration of German thought. The same may become true of the churches. As soon as the war was over, there was an immediate religious revival in postwar Germany—partly due, no doubt, to the desolation of mind caused by total defeat, and to the resulting search for consolation. The churches were the only institutions which retained any vitality after the lost war. In conferences held in 1945 at Fulda and Treysa, the Roman Catholic and Protestant churches undertook to examine their performances during the Nazi era. This may well have given them cause for reflection. Although both groups produced men who offered gallant resistance to nazism, the Roman Catholic Church had signed a concordat with the Germans in 1933, under which priests offered up weekly prayers for the Third Reich, while the Protestants had followed the Lutheran practice of absolute obedience to the state for too long a time. Leading Lutherans and other Protestants, however, were at least prepared to point out in 1945 that there had been a failure to "defend truth unto death"—a phrase used by Pastor Martin Niemöller, one of the foremost leaders of resistance to Hitler.

The churches were generally very full in the first postwar years. Crowding has been less apparent lately, and more than one Roman Catholic bishop has complained bitterly of the churches' emptiness. This is probably due most of all to the materialistic spirit of the present age. But the churches may have missed one opportunity by their failure to interest themselves in social affairs and to come closer to the people in their daily lives. The Evangelicals—the members of the major Protestant churches, which merged in 1948—have been preoccupied with preserving unity across the Iron Curtain frontier that runs through the middle of Germany. (The Roman Catholic Church is not affected to the same degree by this problem, for only about 10 per cent of East German Christians are Catholics.) The Evangelicals produced at least one man who had much to say on the subject of the moral regeneration of the German people: the late Otto Dibelius, the strong-willed Bishop of Berlin and Brandenburg. Dibelius also vigorously opposed the encroachments of Communist-sponsored atheism in East Germany.

APART from moral regeneration, the Germans have had to adjust their views on a wide variety of subjects. Other European nations have had to modify their thinking at times, but none so radically as post-Nazi Germany. One result of this is very apparent. It can be argued that in modern times no nation's creative powers have suffered a greater setback than have those of Germany. For creative performance springs from the interaction of order and revolt, of belief and counterbelief, of conflicting ideas and enthusiasms. But under the wet-nursing of Allied occupation, West Germany evolved the dullest, the least imaginative of utilitarian outlooks.

Utilitarianism in turn brings standard products. The middle-aged, middle-class German is one of them—comporting himself decently in public, wearing discreetly correct clothes, paying his taxes, observing an exact code of formal politeness and possessing a holy horror of falling foul of the law. The German big businessman is another such product—more flamboyant and less inhibited, characteristically wearing a Krefeld necktie (designed from English club colors), building an aquarium into one side of his drawing room, only now beginning to overcome a tendency to isolate himself from the rest of the community. Yet another type is the German aristocrat, if he has retained his estates and capital—remote from nearly everyone except his social equals and his employees, unwittingly asocial and aimless, and too cozily at home with the names that are listed in the *Almanach de Gotha,* the famous registry of nobility.

SUCH people help make up a society which seems strange to Americans or Englishmen brought up to regard their own communities as organic and soundly based. One by-product of this society is the cleavage between age groups as well as classes. Government until recently has been conducted to an unusual degree by old men, a situation which has caused a younger group of parliamentarians in the *Länder* as well as in Bonn to become increasingly disgruntled. The same has been true of industrial leadership, although the picture there is beginning to change more quickly. In general, there has been a disinclination to give youth their fair share in running the community.

It is hard to say how much West German youth have resented this. For the young people's chief characteristic is an extreme reserve. This may not be immediately noticeable. The tastes of German youth seem to be similar to those of young people elsewhere. Young Germans are as active physically as ever they were: they play their games with zest; they are inveterate campers, hikers and travelers. In this respect they are like the members of the *Wandervogel* movement just before World War I, but they are more internationally minded. They have a strong urge to see something of the life of other countries.

Their intellectual stature is less evident. In general, those who are old enough to have experienced the war lack a certain imagination and seem bound by a steady concentration on material objectives. Another generation, however, is presently reaching maturity, unfettered by any taint of war guilt or memories of hunger or terror. These young Germans, whose most vociferous members are university students, are increasingly opposed to a system that appears to have no place in it for them. Yet the depth of their disaffection is unclear. Students did riot in Berlin, Munich and other cities in 1968, but the riots may say more about the appallingly overcrowded and hopelessly outmoded West German universities than about the real mood of the students themselves.

One thing is certain about young people in West Germany—the vast majority of them reject the traditional ideas about German grandeur and glory and about an overbearing German role in Europe, and they are skeptical about any "mission" other than the modest one of being a loyal partner to the western democracies. Although dueling has been revived in some universities, the old brutality is out of fashion. So are fanaticism and racial lunacy.

IT is not at all sure what young Germans will decide about the future of Germany and of Europe. A number of members of the older generation, at least those over 45, believe hopefully in German reunification, in the inviolability of West Berlin in the meantime and in the inalienable right of the German refugees from beyond the Oder to see their old homes someday. Young Germans are more flexible in their ideas, although many of them ardently share such feelings. Their influence will begin to be felt when younger men are at the political helm. One trend which may become evident then will be the desire of young people to explore the feelings of their fellows in East Germany. But the possibility of this remains, for the present, beyond their reach.

At the University of Göttingen, founded in 1737, the late Professor Kurt Latte holds a seminar on Aristophanes' "The Frogs."

Challenges for Ancient Institutions

No prouder traditions exist in Germany than those of education and religion. It was here that compulsory education originated, as well as the great universities on which those of the U.S. were fashioned. Here too the Protestant Reformation was born and the Counter Reformation won major successes. Today school and church wrestle with fresh problems: the travails of brethren behind the Iron Curtain, the difficulties of teaching ways of free thought to a new age.

THE CHURCHES *continue to be a major force*

LUTHERAN CLERGY, led by the late Bishop Dibelius of Berlin (*left*), leave the St. Lamberti Church in Oldenburg. There are 45 million German Protestants.

OUTDOOR MASS is celebrated (*opposite*) in front of Munich's City Hall. Of the country's nearly 30 million Catholics, 90 per cent are in West Germany.

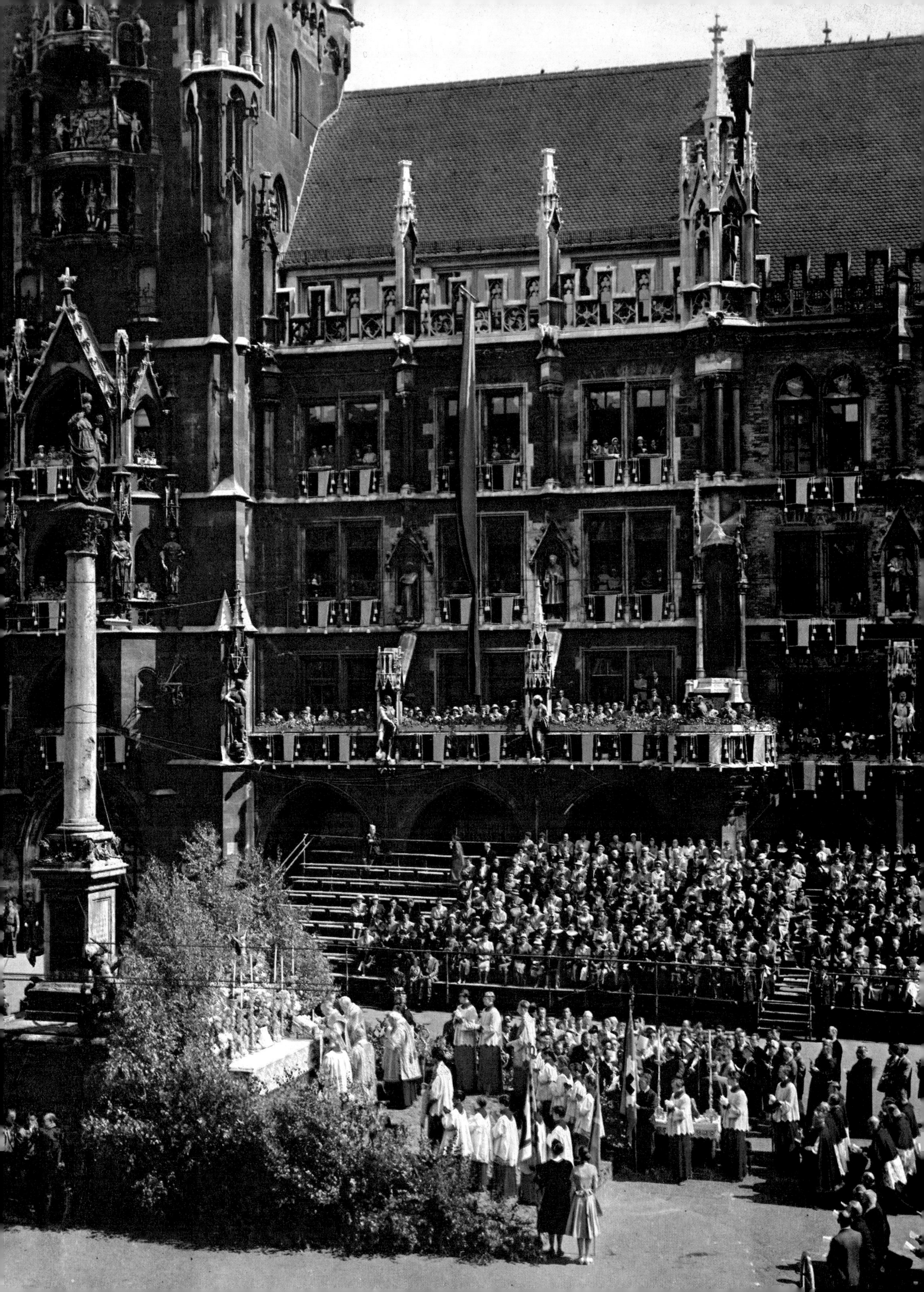

REFURBISHED *in t*

MUNICH CAFE, one of the city's mo
than 1,000 eating and drinking e
tablishments, provides businessmen

postwar years, the cities of Germany today bustle with a new style of living

leasant spot for a tea break (*left*). Half-destroyed in World War II, Munich has since been largely rebuilt.

THRONGED STREET in Frankfurt reflects the city's rebirth as a transportation and financial center (*above*). The Eschenheimer Tower (*background*) is one of the few surviving reminders of Frankfurt's prewar medieval look.

ABSTRACTIONIST, the painter Fritz Winter pauses between canvases. His forceful work established him as a leader of the postwar generation of German artists.

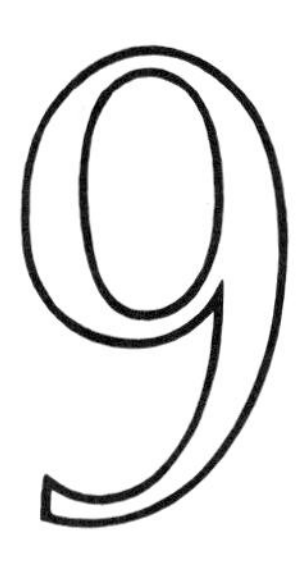

A Resurgence of Intellect

A veneration of cultural achievement may well be one of the most deeply ingrained components of the German character. "Works . . . are of themselves immortal," the 19th Century German philosopher Schopenhauer once wrote, "and especially if they are written, can survive for all time." Veneration of *Kultur* may even be a more potent characteristic than the well-known German sense of order. For the word means so much to so many Germans: the attainment of high scholastic standards, the formal knowledge of the arts, the possession of university degrees or of professorial titles and a consuming interest in the things of the mind.

In his book *The Germans: Double History of a Nation*, Emil Ludwig suggested that the legendary Faust (the erring mortal who was tempted by the devil and whom both the English dramatist Christopher Marlowe and the German poet Johann Wolfgang von Goethe took as the central character for a drama) has been "the great symbol of the German soul, the living witness of why that soul never finds peace." Ludwig calls Faust "the ever-questing German, never resting, forever soaring . . . and never sufficient unto himself." He further relates the character of Faust to the dualism of the Germanic spirit. Faust had an immense capacity for both joy and misery, for goodness and wickedness, for doubt and certainty, for knowledge of redemption and a disbelief in being able to attain it. So has the German, or at least a great many Germans. It was certainly no coincidence that so many German soldiers carried copies of Goethe's *Faust* in their knapsacks during World War I. There were, it must be said, few copies of *Faust* in the duffels of the soldiers of World War II; the Hitler generation had not been taught to read. It is, however, worthy of note that there have been many productions of *Faust* in postwar Germany, and it is perhaps equally noteworthy that the emphasis has shifted of late: the central figure is no longer Faust himself, the futile searcher for truth and love, but his nihilistic companion, the skeptical, ironic Mephistopheles.

The Faust legend is almost certainly a part of the German enigma, whereby a single nation has produced artists, composers, philosophers, thinkers and poets in profusion—as well as Hitler, the most terrible mass-murderer in human history. Just as there have been evil effects, so there can be no doubt that there is a great deal in the cultural world for which humanity should thank the ever-searching Faust. The German achievement in the world of the intellect is a magnificent one.

THE names of Germans who have made individual contributions are legion. One need only mention the painters Albrecht Dürer, Mathias Grünewald and Paul Klee; the scientists Alexander von Humboldt, Johannes Kepler, Wilhelm Röntgen, Max Planck and Albert Einstein; the composers George Frederick Handel, Johann Sebastian Bach, Ludwig van Beethoven, Johannes Brahms, Richard Strauss and Richard Wagner; the poets Goethe, Heinrich Heine and Johann Friedrich von Schiller; and the philosophers Friedrich Nietzsche, Georg Hegel and Immanuel Kant. And, for impact upon the world, one must add the name Karl Marx.

INDISPUTABLY, the output has been uneven. Ludwig said: "Whenever the Reich was strong and united it starved the spirit." This is only one among many curiosities in German history which cannot be easily explained. But it may well be that German energies, when canalized by authority, have been diverted primarily into economic gain and military conquest. The dualism of the German character has usually brought with it an instinctive surrender of individuality to the needs and demands of the state. More than any other European, the German has seemed capable of switching from romanticism to materialism—and back again—at different periods of history. The country has never had a springtime in which political and spiritual values have matured together, or in which creative genius has been synonymous with political progress.

Such a springtime could not possibly have occurred in the immediate postwar years, although in retrospect an observer can see that the subsequent cultural revival of West Germany had its roots in that period. From the start, intellectual life in East Germany was hamstrung by censorship, by the Communist demand for spiritual conformity, and by a rejection of all artistic forms which communism finds difficult to understand or impossible to digest. As late as 1963, while glimmerings of artistic rebirth were visible not only in the Soviet satellites but in the Soviet Union itself, East German boss Walter Ulbricht felt compelled to condemn "abstractionism, formalism and various forms of bourgeois decadence because they are incompatible with the development of realistic performance." Ulbricht added that even some Soviet literature was a bit too revisionist.

It would not, however, be correct to say that all cultural life has ceased in East Germany. In the immediate postwar years the East Berlin Opera was as good as, or better than, anything in the Federal Republic. More recently, it has been outclassed by West Berlin's German Opera, as well as by the Munich and Hamburg companies. But East German theaters, which initially concentrated on safe, traditional productions of the classics, today put on daringly provocative interpretations such as Peter Hacks's renderings of Aristophanes into modern terms, emphasizing the ancient Greek playwright's social satire and cynical pessimism.

In West Germany right after the war there appeared to be a striking lack of creative impulse—the result perhaps of the intellectual limbo imposed on Germany by the war and the numbing effect of material want suffered during the postwar period. Only recently have the country's young intellectuals passionately begun to pick up and carry forward the cultural trends that were so abruptly stifled in the 1930s.

The contrast between West Germany during the first decade after 1945 and the Germany of the Weimar Republic was remarkable. Consider the intellectual achievements of Weimar Germany! It was an era of mingled hope and frustration, of strong passions and much misery. It was an amoral period, in which Berlin earned a worldwide reputation for loose living and each year sprouted a fresh crop of political murders, nationalist conspiracies, and bitter interclass and interparty feuds.

THIS era could never have produced the reflectiveness of Goethe, the grandeur of Bach or the majesty of Beethoven. But the era produced a great deal. Oswald Spengler and Thomas Mann are names that recall breadth of vision allied to mastery of technique. Nor were these two the only outstanding writers of their time. Post-1945 Germany would have been hard put to match Erich Maria Remarque's *All Quiet on the Western Front,* Alfred Döblin's *Berlin Alexanderplatz* or Robert Musil's *The Man Without Qualities.* It seems to have thrown up no single poet of the stature of Stefan George nor a single philosopher who had so wide an impact as Martin Heidegger, whose existentialist philosophy anticipated Jean Paul Sartre and Albert Camus by two decades.

Weimar Germany produced Walter Gropius, Mies van der Rohe and the Bauhaus school of architecture. Germany before World War I had given rise to an Expressionist school of painting, with Klee, George Grosz, Franz Marc and Emil Nolde as its leaders. After the war it produced the composer Paul Hindemith, the instrumentalists Walter Gieseking and Wilhelm Backhaus, and the conductors Wilhelm Furtwängler and Otto Klemperer. The Berlin theater was pre-eminent in Europe; Max Weber had started new trends in sociology; Einstein and Planck were still the most important figures of their day in physics.

POSSIBLY the most striking contrast of all between post-1919 and post-1945 Germany was to be found in the film industry. In the earlier period there were stars like Marlene Dietrich, Emil Jannings and Conrad Veidt, and outstanding directors like Fritz Lang and G. W. Pabst. The industry produced a host of internationally hailed masterpieces such as *The Blue Angel* and *The Cabinet of Dr. Caligari.*

By comparison, the early years after World War II were rather barren. In the mid-1950s, about 110 full-length entertainment films—none of them particularly memorable—were being made each year. That number fell off to 34 in 1964, and the bulk of the output seemed to consist of remakes of B-class, Hollywood westerns of the 1940s' genre. The late 1960s, however, witnessed a whole new phenomenon—the advent of young, enthusiastic experimentalists whose movies revitalized the moribund industry. Box office successes have been registered despite the presence of unknown performers and unusual themes. Ordinary neighborhood movie houses have been closing by the thousands, but art cinemas, thanks to a fresh approach to filmmaking, are prospering.

German television is noted for its outstanding quality. It presents classic as well as modern plays, commissions its own dramas and forthrightly examines contemporary issues. It provides a supplementary income for some of the country's most controversial and original minds. For the cost of slightly over a dollar a month, program subscribers are provided with a minimum of commercials and a maximum of enlightenment and entertainment. Economic prosperity has been good to the television industry: whereas the head of the German household once spent long hours at the local beer hall, he is now content to settle comfortably with his beer in front of his television set.

ANOTHER cultural field which is thriving is the theater. While there has been an acknowledged dearth of dramatic writing talent (perhaps because many of the dramatists are working in television), there has been plenty of interest in the performing arts themselves. There are some 200 theaters in West Germany and together they put on more than 5,000 productions of plays, operas, operettas and occasional concerts per year. Roughly 80 per cent of their seats are filled night after night.

Admittedly, part of this takes place because tickets are inexpensive—the Federal Republic grants an annual subsidy of $75 million to the German theater. Moreover, the motivation of the average German theatergoer is often extraneous to the play he attends. Along with shiny new cars and foreign travel, *Kultur* remains a password of social respectability—and, incidentally, is for that very reason an object of derision for many of Germany's most outspoken intellectuals who have lately taken up the cry of "anti-*Kultur.*" The occasional evening at the theater is part and parcel of the search for status: *"Es gehört zum guten Ton,"* runs a German saying—"It's a matter of good tone." An attitude like this may not make for exciting audiences, but it does not obviate the possibility that people will be genuinely moved by what they see in the theater, and the Germans see some of the most provocative dramas to be found anywhere: *The Zoo Story* and *The Death of Bessie Smith,* the first plays written by the American dramatist Edward Albee *(Who's Afraid of Virginia Woolf?),* had their initial productions in West Germany; Albert Bessler, deputy director of West Berlin's Schiller Theater, was responsible for giving Samuel Beckett's *Waiting for Godot* its first major production; and Erwin Piscator of the West Berlin Volksbüne first produced *The Deputy,* Rolf Hochhuth's controversial indictment of Pope Pius XII's actions during the Nazi persecution of the Jews.

If there was a long hiatus in German writing, it may have been caused by the baneful influence that the Nazi era exercised on the arts. Joseph Goebbels made his gigantic bonfires of "subversive" books, ones by foreign authors as well as by Germans. His object was to choke off independent thought, and he succeeded all too well. Moreover, Hitler regarded himself as an arbiter of artistic taste. He banned men like Willi Baumeister and Karl Hofer from painting, and condemned as "degenerate" the artistic ideas of the Bauhaus group.

HITLER introduced his own ideas into architecture, and these took shape in huge stadiums, monumental halls and public palaces with neoclassical trappings, Grecian colonnades, Roman pediments and monstrous statuary, all of which were somehow intended to presage the "Greater German Reich." He also had grandiose plans to remodel Berlin as the center of Europe. His attempt to prove Germanic superiority by allying nazism with classicism stifled the cultural life of Germany and turned the clock back on all contemporary movements.

Hitler struck his heaviest blow at the arts and sciences by persecuting the Jews. What the loss of the Jews has meant cannot be truly imagined outside Germany. German Jewish talent had flourished in the theater, in the cinema industry, in music, science, literature and painting. By 1938 the Jews had been virtually eliminated from the country's cultural life. At the

GREAT MEN OF GERMAN CULTURE
Some noted personalities from a rich cultural past are shown in areas identified with their names. Further information on each can be found in the Appendix.
Felix Mendelssohn, composer
Johannes Brahms, composer
(Hamburg)
Martin Luther, reformer (Wittenberg)
Thomas Mann, writer (Lübeck)
Georg Hegel, philosopher
Bertolt Brecht, playwright (Berlin)
Johann von Goethe, poet
Johann von Schiller, poet
Friedrich Nietzsche, philosopher (Weimar)
Ludwig van Beethoven, composer (Bonn)
George Frederick Handel, composer (Halle)
Immanuel Kant, philosopher (Königsberg, off map)
Heinrich Heine, poet (Göttingen)
Johann Sebastian Bach, composer
Robert Schumann, composer (Leipzig)
Johann Gutenberg, printer (Mainz)
Richard Wagner, composer (Bayreuth)
Albrecht Dürer, painter (Nuremberg)
Lucas Cranach the Elder, painter (Kronach)
Mathias Grünewald, painter (Isenheim)
Richard Strauss, composer (Munich)
Hans Holbein the Elder, painter
Hans Holbein the Younger, painter
(Augsburg)

end of the war the 30,000 or so Jews remaining in Germany could not bring back their unique inventiveness of mind to the arid wasteland which Hitler left behind. The Jewish communities in Germany today are pitifully small, aging and unsure. In Sweden, however, Nelly Sachs, a German-born Jew who fled from the Nazis in 1940 when she was already in her fifties, has managed eloquently to convey the hurt suffered by her people. For her haunting poetry, alive with image and allegory, she was awarded the Nobel Prize in 1966.

After 1945 young Germans had to be informed who the great figures in German literature were. They had barely heard of Thomas Mann or Franz Kafka. But ignorance apart, they were profoundly shocked by total war, total defeat and foreign occupation of their divided country. A whole system had been swept away, and under the poultice of Allied occupation nothing could quickly be put into its place save the outward forms of democracy. For German thinkers and artists seemed to find no obvious focus after 1945.

THE protest of post-1945 German intellectuals—of the survivors of the Weimar era and of a new generation which was relatively barren of thought—could have been directed against two things: the mistakes of the past and the materialism of the present. German intellectuals should have played the principal role in performing an autopsy of the past, as well as in fighting the fungus of cynicism and self-interest which has coated the country's "economic miracle." In recent years some have indeed tried, and it is fair to say that a literary revival is in full swing in West Germany.

The success in the 1960s of three writers in particular—Günter Grass, Heinrich Böll and Uwe Johnson—signaled the change. The solid achievement of these men represented the fulfilled promise of a handful of serious writers, most of them young and linked with a maverick literary movement founded in 1947 and known as Group 47. Group 47's members have persistently tried to probe beneath economic prosperity and to examine the uneasy past. What lends urgency to their literary inquiry is the parallel most of them see between the new smugness and materialism they believe exist in contemporary Germany and the self-seeking spirit that permeated Germany under Hitler.

Most impressive of the new literary crop is Günter Grass, possibly the most inventive talent to be heard from anywhere since the war. A sprawling bear of a man, Grass was born the son of a grocer in 1927. His first novel, *The Tin Drum,* which was published in 1959, employs every technique from realism to surrealism, every tone from a whisper to a howl. Its central character is a dwarf named Oskar Matzerath, who witnesses in a series of tragicomic details the rise of nazism. When Oskar's father joins the party and feels himself becoming a hero of blood and iron, he is deflated when he has trouble acquiring a brown shirt to go with his uniform.

To make Oskar's odyssey say more than Oskar himself, Grass interweaves his story with symbols and takes off on flights of incantatory eloquence. Evil is a black witch who resides, according to a German children's song, "in you, you, you." There is a link between evil and self-gratification, Grass seems to be telling us, as in this passage, which describes the killing of Oskar's father by Russian troops and the falling of his body across the path of some ants on a journey to a broken sugar sack: "The ants found themselves facing a new situation, but, undismayed by the detour, soon built a new highway round the doubled-up Matzerath, for the sugar that trickled out of the burst sack had lost none of its sweetness while Marshal Rokossovsky was occupying . . . Danzig."

THE senior figure in Group 47 is Heinrich Böll, a veteran novelist. His major work, *Billiards at Half Past Nine,* tells the story of an architect who spends the war as a demolition expert. In disgust with local churchmen and townsfolk who are more concerned with preserving national monuments than with saving the lives of Nazi victims, he blows up a church designed by his own father, also an architect. The architect's mother rebels against the complacency of the townsfolk, too; she attempts to thrust herself into freight cars bound for Auschwitz to call them to public attention. Eventually confined to an asylum, the mother recognizes the real enemy—not the Nazis, who personify the known power of evil, but respectability, which would rather look the other way than cause a fuss.

Like Böll and Grass, Uwe Johnson, a writer who grew up during the Nazi years (he was born in 1934), views today's Germany as the dangerous and corrupt legacy of yesterday. But his main target is less the confrontation of the past than the misunderstood present. An East German who came to the West in 1960, he seems to offer Germans the gloomiest of choices. Virtually plotless, his books make the point that East Germany is a police state, less oppressive than the West thinks, but nevertheless no place to live. West Germany, though relatively free, is poisoned with smug, forgetful materialism and a lack of purpose.

BOLL, Johnson and Grass clearly do not fit into any neat school of literature. What they and the other Group 47 writers most closely resemble is a kind of self-elected national conscience for Germany. Eloquently and angrily they argue that the destruction of individual character (and of nations) begins with the tiniest indifference, the smallest act of cowardice, the most microscopic compromise. But the point must also be made that most writers today still seem to fail to capture the West German reality, that they are frequently obsessed with the guilt-ridden past.

This has never been more shockingly portrayed than in *The Investigation,* a drama by Peter Weiss based on the Auschwitz war-crimes trial. Weiss, another gifted and outspoken member of Group 47, is perhaps best known abroad for his wildly witty play about the French polemicist Marat and the Marquis de Sade.

Heinrich Böll, no depicter of prettiness in his own novels, tried to analyze the reasons in the magazine *Der Monat* in 1965. "Why," he inquired, "is there no gay novel on this flourishing country? . . . This is a sad country without sadness. It has delegated its sadness, pushed it over the eastern border and doesn't yet know that the political is only at the surface, a thin crust and the most vulnerable of all layers. . . ."

In painting, there has been a considerable rebirth. Modern art has found increasing acceptance throughout West Germany. In 1955 Munich possessed only four galleries devoted to contemporary art; by the late 1960s the number had grown to more than 50. There is considerable interest in the Blaue Reiter and Brücke groups, whose Expressionist style was once the main target of Hitler's ire. There is also a great deal of interest in the work of older artists who were also forbidden to work by the Nazis and who came to the fore only after 1945. These artists include the sculptor Bernhard Heiliger and the painters Hans Hartung, Oskar Kokoschka, Hap Grieshaber and Fritz Winter. Yet the main subjects of interest—shared by both the countless galleries and by the prestigious Documenta Show which takes place in Kassel—are the new painters and sculptors who started their careers long after the Nazis vanished. Among them is Düsseldorf's Gruppe Zero, whose members Otto Piene, Heinz Mack and Guenther Uecker are to be counted among the founding fathers of kinetic and op art. There is also the young painter Horst Antes, a master of color, the post-Expressionist portraitist Hans Platschek, and the sculptors Norbert Kricke and O. H. Hajek. These and many others are providing the German scene with a new liveliness which rivals that of the productive 1920s.

THE picture has not been quite so bright musically. Carl Orff, Werner Egk, Hans Werner Henze and Karlheinz Stockhausen are composers of note, but in general Germany has produced little of musical importance in recent years. It has, however, produced some notable performers. Karl Richter's Bach ensemble in

Munich is one of the world's best. The late Wieland Wagner, grandson of Richard, added new dimensions to opera by brilliant staging of his grandfather's works in Bayreuth.

IF intellectual life is stirring in the Federal Republic, where intellectual independence was in abeyance for a mere 12 years, what of East Germany, where freedom of thought has not existed for nearly 30 years? Boris Pasternak's *Dr. Zhivago* has given the lie to those who maintain that creative endeavor cannot come to anything under Communist dictatorship. Yet *Zhivago* and Pasternak were products of the Russian mind and of its ability, even under an authoritarian regime, to search for critical and constructive standards. It is doubtful whether there can ever be any literary achievement like *Zhivago* in a Communist-controlled Germany. The Ulbricht regime was imposed on its subjects by an alien authority. Although a few independent souls such as the poet Wolfgang Biermann and the philosopher Ernst Havemann are gaining followers, intellectual conviction remains a rare commodity.

It is not surprising that hundreds of East German intellectuals have sought refuge in the Federal Republic, although some of them have found the creed of materialism so strong there that they have done little work. Two of East Germany's most respected minds—the philosopher Ernst Bloch and the literary historian Hans Mayer—have made it to the West, Bloch to teach at the university at Tübingen, Mayer to work at the Technische Hochschule in Hanover. Since 1958, when the Communists reorganized the university system, more than 1,700 other university and college lecturers and professors have fled from East to West Germany. Nor is it surprising that Bertolt Brecht has remained so solitary a giant in the realm of creative work in East Germany, or that theater tickets there are becoming more difficult to sell (in the 1959-1960 season, total theater attendance in East Germany was 16 million, as against 12 million in 1965-1966).

It is small wonder that East Germany, while prolific in dialecticians, has produced few artists of truly independent outlook since the war. Anna Seghers has written novels and short stories; Arnold Zweig, already 58 years old at the end of the war, probably did his best writing earlier. Obviously greater than theirs has been the achievement of Brecht, who died in East Germany in 1956. His *Threepenny Opera* ran for 2,611 performances in New York before closing in 1961, and several other of his works have been enthusiastically received there since.

Brecht's sardonic, often vitriolic wit may have been a screen behind which he hid his own true feelings. But it may have reflected the true character of the man, burned into his brain by the ironies of his existence. For nothing could have been more ironic than that this arch-opponent of the superauthority of all established order should have had to end his days in an authoritarian state. Brecht may have developed his own uncertainties of mind in his last years—his anti-military play, *Schweik in the Second World War,* with its somewhat naïve pillorying of Hitler, suggested this. Much of his best work was done before 1945; a contributory factor may have been the doubts which he is alleged to have developed about the East German regime.

IT is difficult to visualize a creative intellectual life emerging in East Germany as long as the country is ruled by what is essentially an alien Communist regime. The outlook for West Germany is very different. For its people have begun to come to terms with their own past. Two decades of dictatorship and military occupation seem to have had a temporarily stultifying effect on German minds. This effect is wearing off. It may well be that a younger generation growing up in West Germany will be able to evolve its own philosophy and forms of self-expression and will benefit from closer contact with other nations and their ideas. The rebuilding of self-reliance, the discarding of dogma, the desire to inject spiritual values into a materialistic existence—these may become the operative influences in an intellectual revival in West Germany.

A pictorial biography, this detail from a panel on the life of Christ is by a 15th Century artist known only as the Master of Cologne.

Brief, Glorious Age in Art

The Renaissance flourished briefly in Germany. But the paintings produced by such masters as Dürer and Holbein in the golden 15th Century have never been surpassed by Germans. Not until Expressionism arrived half a century ago did German painting once again win world-wide recognition and acclaim.

CHRISTIAN HUMANISM *inspired the works of the earlier masters*

"**BIRTH OF CHRIST**" (*opposite*) by the great Albrecht Dürer (1471-1528) exemplifies the artist's lifelong concern with the relationship of man to God and the universe.

"**AGONY IN GETHSEMANE**" by Wolf Huber (1490-1553) depicts Christ's spiritual strength triumphing over His fear as Roman soldiers draw near and the disciples sleep.

CRUCIFIXION, painted by Mathias Grünewald (c. 1470-1528), dominates the exterior of the Isenheim Altarpiece. Commissioned by the monks of St. Anthony, it is regarded as one of Germany's greatest works of religious art.

NOTE OF HOPE that bespeaks the painter's faith leavens the scene: just to the right of the Cross are John the Baptist and his prophecy, "He must increase. . . ." In the panels are St. Anthony (*left*) and St. Sebastian (*right*).

PORTRAIT OF A MERCHANT, this painting of George Giesze demonstrates the skill with which Hans Holbein the Younger (1493-1543) captured physiognomy.

PORTRAIT OF A PRINCESS, Elizabeth of Saxony (*opposite*), by Lucas Cranach the Younger (1515-1586) catches the demureness and petulance of the subject.

NEW MOVEMENTS *have revitalized painting in the 20th Century*

BOLDNESS OF STYLE dominates *Women on the Street* (*opposite*), which was painted just before World War I by Ernst Ludwig Kirchner, an early German Expressionist.

MASTERY OF COLOR and vigor of line characterize *The King*, which Max Beckmann produced before World War II in his highly subjective mode of Expressionism.

SATIRE on hypocrisy i George Grosz's inten in this 1918 work (*right*) which shows a raucou mob at the funeral of a poet who sought truth

TENDER PIETY fills Emil Nolde's *Christ Among the Children*, produced in 1910, five years after the founding of the German Expressionist movement.

OUTSIZED FIGURES, as in *Couple with Bird* (*right*), mark the work of Horst Antes, a young painter who says, "I am trying to make man perfect again."

BAR

IN MEDITATION, a man and a lederhosen-clad young boy pass a quiet moment near a medieval castle alongside the peaceful banks of a Bavarian mountain stream.

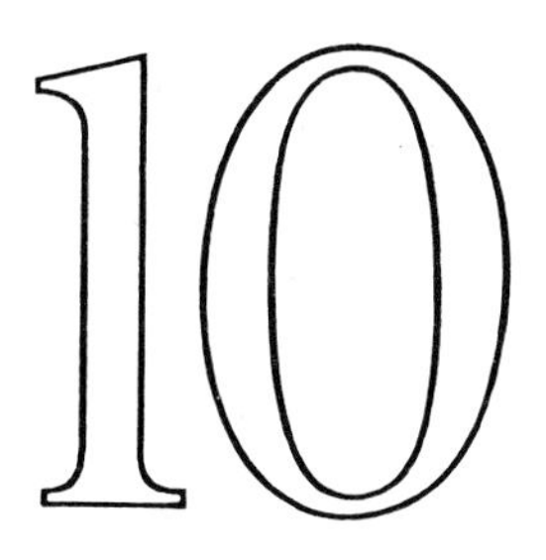

The Unsettled and Perilous Future

"FROM such a defeat," the German writer Ernst Jünger said in 1945, "one does not recover any longer, as peoples formerly recovered after [great battles like] Jena or . . . Sedan. Such a defeat marks a turning-point in the life of nations."

The defeat of 1945 had all the appearances of a catastrophe, and one which was the logical outcome of nazism. The Nazi era was not an isolated episode in the history of the German people, and German historians who pretend that it was are doing a disservice to Germans who are anxious to find out about their past. Hitler's dream of a *Grossdeutsches Reich* was no more than the romantic projection of visions held by Germans for generations.

It may seem academic today whether the Germans should bear the whole blame for World War II, or whether the victor nations of 1919 should shoulder a large part of it for imposing so harsh a peace treaty as the one signed at Versailles. But one aspect of the question of blame should not be forgotten. While millions of Americans and Englishmen in the 1920s and 1930s were praying that there would be no more wars, the German people were being guided by their intellectuals into very different channels of thought. In 1924 the philosopher Oswald Spengler wrote, "The fact that we as Germans can finally hate is one of the few developments in our time which can assure our future."

It is hard to imagine how an intelligent man could write such rubbish. But by doing so, men like Spengler made their own contributions to the rise of the National Socialists and the ruin of their country. Moreover, their views were in line with those of the great majority of their compatriots. As a present-day German historian, Ludwig Dehio, has written, "The defeat was ascribed to the deceit of our enemies, and to errors and treason at home. We brooded over our defeat, but in order to prove to ourselves that it was undeserved, not to understand why it was deserved."

ONE hopeful portent for Germany's future is that today the vast majority of the German people no longer thinks in terms of revenge. Today the German echoes the American and Englishman of 40 years ago. The phrase "no more wars" is never far from his mind and is often on his lips. History may decide that one factor contributed importantly to this change: the overwhelming repudiation, through the 1945 defeat, of the militaristic spirit which had grown so alarmingly after 1871. For it was the militaristic ideal of discipline and devotion to duty that helped Hitler most in exhorting the German people to back him in his conquest and enslavement of Europe. Had this spirit survived, the building of a new German state might have been as difficult in the 1940s as it was after 1919.

What other hopeful signs for the future are there? One is the close association today of three fourths of the German people with the other nations of western Europe. For more than a hundred years—until 1945—German thought moved progressively faster away from the traditions of western European civilization. Many of Germany's intellectuals moved out of the mainstream of European intellectual life. Their reflexes, their prejudices, even their considered views were conditioned by nationalistic and narrowly parochial feelings. Even some so-called German liberals at the beginning of this century believed in the Kaiser as the only true emperor, in the creation of a huge navy and in a German empire in the East.

SINCE 1949 the Federal Republic has been trying to work its passage as a loyal partner in the western alliance. Its government has backed almost every plan for European economic and political integration. Adenauer was shocked when France rejected the first plan for a European army in which soldiers of member countries would serve in international units, a program Germany supported. In NATO the West Germans have been good partners, scrupulously fulfilling their obligations; they have also shown a readiness to mediate (without forcing their mediation on anybody) between the nations of the Common Market and the European nations outside it. They supported Britain's unsuccessful application to join the Market. They balked at only one European plan—that advanced by General de Gaulle for creating a European Third Force, an inner ring within NATO that would become increasingly independent of the United States. Although he generally saw eye to eye with De Gaulle, Adenauer gave the Third Force plan no encouragement, and it has had none since.

The integration of West Germany into western Europe is admirable. It is not just that the 12 West German divisions in NATO help to shore up the bulwark against the further advance of communism, or that U.S. and British troops in Germany are accepted amicably as the principal element of that bulwark. The West Germans are returning today to western Europe—where they want to belong. The chief beneficiary will be Europe itself. Next will come the underdeveloped countries of the world, which must look to Europe for technical, financial and moral aid. The Germans are aware of this need. In the 1960s they spent an average of almost $500 million every year on aid to underdeveloped countries.

The postwar economic miracle is not in itself a guarantee of a more settled German future, but the gradual acceptance of democracy is. More than 20 years after the war, however, it is still not possible to say that a majority of West Germans have a positive faith in the democratic process. For such a conviction means essentially the individual's positive faith in his own independent judgment—something that many Germans have lacked in the past and cannot develop in a hurry. But conditions have at least been created in West Germany for the free, spontaneous formation and expression of opinions.

A spirit of individuality, as opposed to one of anarchy of mind, is becoming more prevalent today. Ordinary citizens write to the newspapers and say what they really think. The papers themselves show a refreshing independence of outlook, offering criticism more freely than ever before and defending the liberties of the press jealously. The old German fear of the *Obrigkeiten*, the powers-that-be, is draining away. Those *Obrigkeiten* are themselves losing their officiousness and leavening their sense of duty with politeness. Here again the disappearance of the old German worship of the state should have healthy results. The rigidity of the Hitlerite *Einheitstaat,* or unified state, has been replaced by a federalism which has given Germans time and room in which to breathe. The German tendency to rely on strong government, even on the undue authority of a single man, still exists. But the postwar years have restrained and modified it.

Yet there remains a host of awkward question marks. Shortly before he defected to East Germany in 1954, Otto John, the head of the West German security services, told a foreign journalist that nothing had "really been settled" in Germany. There is still some truth in this remark. The Germans have a burgeoning understanding of the true meaning of democracy. But many things continue to be unsettled. The country is still divided. Its eastern frontier is only provisional. Berlin's position is an anomaly. Nevertheless, in West Germany transfers of leadership have been relatively smooth, and the Federal Republic has continued to hold its regular democratic elections. As for East Germany's leadership, no one knows what will happen when Ulbricht dies. That and many other questions remain to be answered. Will the democratic experiment in the West succeed—and the Communist experiment in the East? Will the West Germans reconcile themselves to their present role in western Europe, or will they eventually come to the conclusion that this could hurt Germany's chances of reunification?

The West German people face stresses and strains without number. The Federal Republic will continue to be subjected to persistent, powerful and often insidious Communist pressures. The East German Republic provides an outer bastion from which the Communists can apply pressure against "rump-Germany," as they call the Federal Republic. Soviet leaders have stated openly that they have decided to focus a major effort on defeating the West in the economic arena. Their objectives have also included the splitting up of western Europe, its gradual absorption into the Communist bloc and the capture of the continent's immense industrial potential.

THE German position is peculiarly sensitive because Berlin can be periodically squeezed, because the West Germans are of necessity dependent on their NATO partners and because any power that is in the front line of a cold war is bound to be uncomfortable. The Soviet Union can always play on the military indefensibility of Berlin or threaten to make a separate peace with the East Germans. Communist propaganda in West Germany is unresting; it may easily cost several hundred million marks a year.

West Germans will continue to be gravely concerned by the division of their country. They may become increasingly impatient—though agonizingly unable to affect matters. Their concern was heightened by the waning resistance to communism in East Germany—in good part due to the flight of so many people opposed to the Ulbricht regime. The erection of the Berlin Wall did not ease matters; by halting the manpower drain it made East Germany more self-sufficient and further widened the breach between East and West.

The French coined the phrase, "Nous ne voulons pas mourir pour Königsberg," meaning that they would not fight in a war waged to recover lost German possessions in the East. Even the most ardent German patriot today does not contemplate a hot war to reunify his country—although he sometimes talks about it. Other Europeans would not relish dying for Leipzig and Dresden. They may, in fact, cease to worry about Leipzig and Dresden at all. For there seems little sense in worrying, when only the Soviet Union can grant German unity and when the Soviet Union so plainly does not intend to grant it except on its own unpalatable terms.

DESPITE all these difficulties, many Germans still honestly wish for reunification in peace and freedom, and this sentiment may continue to arouse distrust in the West. Many Frenchmen and Englishmen, for instance, have written off reunification already. They can only foresee a possibility of some sort of confederation of the two German states, of the kind proposed by Ulbricht and Khrushchev. Many Europeans still cherish a resentment against the Germans and remain unconvinced that there is such a thing as German regeneration. Some still fear German military might.

Germans are acutely aware of this lingering distrust in the West. They consequently find it harder to cultivate confident self-reliance in place of occasional cockiness. They therefore are likely to doubt that the western nations are genuinely interested in German reunification. For even Europeans who have no special dislike for the Germans believe that there is something to be said for the perpetuation of the status quo in central Europe. Unfortunately, this view presupposes accepting and making the best of Germany's division.

If the West cannot help, what hopes are left that the division might end? Many Germans yearn vaguely for an internal liberalization in the Soviet Union or hope that the Sino-Soviet split and the Soviet's troubles with its increasingly independent satellites will force it to alter its stand on reunification. But there has been no sign that this is happening. At present, the leaders of the Soviet Union seem merely to have put the German problem on ice, and the Germans themselves have discovered no new road to reunification.

IN a dozen years' time younger men will be playing a big part in ruling both of the German states. In East Germany they may be as closely bound to the Soviet Union as are the men of the Ulbricht regime today. But there is no knowing how a younger generation in West Germany will view its tasks and aims. By the late 1960s, more than half of the population had been born after the Nazi era. Each quadrennial Federal election will bring approximately three million new voters to the polls. By 1973 there will be 13 million people—nearly a third of the electorate—who will barely remember the defeat of 1945. Will this younger generation decide that big risks must be taken to secure German unity? Will it decide that West Germany must content itself with the place it has achieved in the western community? Will it succeed in evolving new, flexible policies—thereby making both of these things possible? Finally, will it find new ideals and a sense of fulfillment, and so build a contented and whole community? Unfortunately, none of these questions can be answered yet. Such is the uncertainty which still confronts the German people.

Young German soldiers visit the graves of World War I dead in a French cemetery. Next page: Art students picnic on the Rhine.

HARSH MEMORIES *continue to plague a much-torn people . . .*

. . . who place their hopes for future quietude in sons and daughters soon

to take over the leadership of a land beset by vast and unsolved problems

Appendix

HISTORICAL DATES

B.C.

c.1000-100 Germanic tribes settle in northern and central Europe

A.D.

9 German victory at Teutoburg Forest halts Roman efforts to colonize beyond the Rhine

c.370 Germanic peoples begin mass infiltration of Roman Empire

378 Goths defeat Romans at Battle of Adrianople

481-511 Clovis of the Franks defeats scattered tribes, establishes a united state on what is now French and German territory

768-814 Reign of Charlemagne (Karl der Grosse), who consolidates and extends the Frankish kingdom

800 Charlemagne crowned "Emperor of the Romans"

843 Charlemagne's empire divided among his grandsons. Louis the German receives eastern Frankish kingdom, nucleus of future German state

936-973 Reign of Otto I. As an ally of the Church he is crowned emperor by Pope John XII, an event which establishes claim of succeeding German kings to title of Holy Roman Emperor

1056-1105 Reign of Henry IV, central figure in the opening stages of the long power struggle between emperors and papacy

1122 Concordat of Worms, which temporarily settles emperor-pope dispute by giving the pope the right to invest high church officials with spiritual powers and the emperor the right to invest them with temporal powers

1152-1190 Reign of Frederick Barbarossa of the Hohenstaufen dynasty, who conquers and Christianizes the Slavs of eastern Germany. Agriculture and industry thrive under him and his immediate successors

1235 At Diet of Mainz Frederick II, grandson of Frederick Barbarossa, establishes a court which is empowered to try all cases except those of the great vassals

1241 Northern German towns organize for protection and trade

1254-1273 The Great Interregnum: struggle over the imperial succession; feuding nobles terrorize the country

1273 Election of Rudolf I, first Hapsburg emperor

1356 Golden Bull, issued by Emperor Charles IV, regulates the imperial succession

1417 Frederick I of the Hohenzollern family, which later rules over Prussia and Germany, is appointed Elector of Brandenburg

1517 The Protestant Reformation begins. Luther nails his 95 theses attacking Church abuses to the door of the Wittenberg church

1519-1558 Reign of Charles V

1521 Diet of Worms, presided over by Charles, issues order for Luther's arrest. In hiding, Luther translates the New Testament into German

1545-1563 Council of Trent codifies Catholic beliefs and doctrine, reforms Church abuses

1546-1547 Schmalkaldic War: Protestant princes and free cities defeated by Catholic Charles V

1555 Peace of Augsburg introduces the principle of *cuius regio, eius religio,* which forces subjects to adopt the religion of their rulers or emigrate elsewhere. Religious wars temporarily halted

1618-1648 Thirty Years' War, a combined religious, political and dynastic struggle, rages across German territory; is settled by Peace of Westphalia, which restricts the power of the Holy Roman Emperor and brings the religious wars to a close

1701 Frederick I of Prussia proclaims his duchy a kingdom

1713-1740 Reign of Frederick William I of Prussia, who organizes a powerful army

1740-1786 Reign of Frederick II (Frederick the Great) of Prussia

1740-1748 War of the Austrian Succession involves Austria and Prussia on opposing sides. Victorious Prussia gains new territories

1756-1763 Seven Years' War. Austria fails to defeat Prussia. Prussian strength mounts

1795 Prussia defeated in war with France

1803-1815 Napoleonic Wars

1806 After defeat by Napoleon at Austerlitz, Francis I of Austria relinquishes title of Holy Roman Emperor. Empire formally dissolved

1807 Defeated again in war with France, Prussia becomes a virtual vassal of Napoleon

1815 Napoleon defeated. Congress of Vienna restores Prussian territories, grants new ones to Prussia and Austria. A federation of German states, including Prussia and Austria, is formed

1848 Revolutions in German states win limited reforms. Metternich forced from power

1862 Otto von Bismarck begins long service as powerful figure in Prussia (later Germany)

1864 Prussia and Austria war successfully against Denmark

1866 Allies split. Prussia wars on and defeats Austria

1871 Germany wins Franco-Prussian War, acquires Alsace-Lorraine. Wilhelm I of Prussia declared German Emperor (Kaiser)

1888-1918 Reign of Kaiser Wilhelm II

1890 Bismarck dismissed

1914-1918 World War I

1918 Kaiser abdicates

1919 Alsace-Lorraine returned to France

1919-1933 Weimar Republic

1923 Hitler's Munich beer-hall *Putsch*

1929-1934 World economic crisis precipitates large-scale unemployment and major depression

1933-1945 Nazi regime, the Third Reich

1933 Hitler appointed Chancellor

1936 Germany remilitarizes the Rhineland. Establishment of the Rome-Berlin axis

1938 Hitler annexes Austria. Munich Pact permits Germany to occupy part of Czechoslovakia

1939 Germany's invasion of Poland starts World War II

1945 Hitler commits suicide in Berlin. War ends

1945 Allied rule: Germany is divided into four occupation zones

1948-1949 Berlin Blockade

1949 Establishment of the Federal Republic (West Germany) and the Democratic Republic (East Germany)

1955 NATO admits West Germany

1957 West Germany joins the European Common Market

1961 Berlin Wall erected

1963 Konrad Adenauer retires as Chancellor of West Germany; Ludwig Erhard succeeds him

1966 Erhard resigns; Kurt Georg Kiesinger and Willy Brandt form a coalition government

1967 Konrad Adenauer dies

FOR FURTHER READING

CHAPTER 1: A PEOPLE OF DISCIPLINE AND ENERGY

Boehle, Bernd, *Handy Guide to Western Germany*. William Sloane Associates, 1956.
Fodor, Eugene, ed., *Germany 1961*. David McKay, 1961.
Ogrizek, Doré, ed., *Germany*. McGraw-Hill, 1956.
Pollock, James K., and Homer L. Thomas, *Germany in Power and Eclipse*. D. Van Nostrand, 1952.
Press and Information Office, Federal Government of Germany, *Facts About Germany*, 1960.
Press and Information Office, Federal Government of Germany, *Germany in a Nutshell*, 1960.
Shepherd, William R., *Historical Atlas*. Barnes & Noble, 1956.

CHAPTER 2: THE UNRESOLVED QUEST FOR UNITY

Barraclough, Geoffrey, *The Origins of Modern Germany*. Macmillan, 1948.
Eyck, Erich, *Bismarck and the German Empire*. Macmillan, 1950.
Flenley, Ralph, *Modern German History*. E. P. Dutton, 1959.
Gooch, George P., *Germany*. Charles Scribner's Sons, 1925.
Kohn, Hans, ed., *German History, Some New German Views*. Beacon Press, 1954.
Pinson, K. S., *Modern Germany; Its History and Civilization*. Macmillan, 1954.
Reinhardt, Kurt F., *Germany: 2000 Years*. Frederick Ungar, 1961.
Shirer, William L., *The Rise and Fall of the Third Reich*. Simon and Schuster, 1960.
Taylor, A.J.P., *Bismarck, the Man and the Statesman*. Alfred A. Knopf, 1955.
Valentin, Veit, *The German People*. Alfred A. Knopf, 1946.

CHAPTER 3: THE CONSTRUCTION OF A STABLE STATE

Cole, Taylor, ed., *European Political Systems*. Alfred A. Knopf, 1959.
Golay, John F., *The Founding of the Federal Republic of Germany*. University of Chicago Press, 1957.
Litchfield, Edward H., and others, *Governing Postwar Germany*. Cornell University Press, 1953.
Weymar, Paul, *Adenauer: His Authorized Biography*. E. P. Dutton, 1957.
Zink, Harold, *The United States in Germany, 1944-1955*. D. Van Nostrand, 1957.

CHAPTER 4: A PROSPERITY REBORN

Davidson, Eugene, *The Death and Life of Germany*. Alfred A. Knopf, 1959.
Muhlen, Norbert, *The Incredible Krupps*. Holt, Rinehart and Winston, 1959.
Pounds, Norman John Greville, *The Ruhr*. Indiana University Press, 1952.
Sasuly, Richard, *I. G. Farben*. Boni & Gaer, 1947.

CHAPTER 5: IN THE SHADOW OF THE SOVIET

Brant, Stefan, *The East German Rising*. Frederick A. Praeger, 1953.
Leonhard, Wolfgang, *Child of the Revolution*. Henry Regnery, 1959.
Nettl, J. P., *The Eastern Zone and Soviet Policy in Germany, 1945-1950*. Oxford University Press, 1951.
Stolper, Wolfgang F., with the assistance of Karl W. Roskamp, *The Structure of the East German Economy*. Harvard University Press, 1960.
Thalheim, Karl C., "Eastern Germany," in Stephen D. Kertesz, ed., *The Fate of East Central Europe*. University of Notre Dame Press, 1956.

CHAPTER 6: A CAPITAL WITHOUT A COUNTRY

Butler, Ewan, *City Divided: Berlin 1955*. Frederick A. Praeger, 1955.
Clay, Lucius D., *Decision in Germany*. Doubleday, 1950.
Press and Information Office of the Land of Berlin, *Berlin, Facts and Figures*, 1960.
Press and Information Office of the Land of Berlin, *Berlin—Fate and Mission*, 1959.
Riess, Curt, *The Berlin Story*. Dial Press, 1952.

CHAPTER 7: THE PEACEABLE SMALL MAN

Abel, Theodore Fred, *Why Hitler Came Into Power*. Prentice-Hall, 1938.
Görlitz, Walter, *History of the German General Staff, 1657 to 1945*. Frederick A. Praeger, 1953.
Morgan, John H., *Assize of Arms; The Disarmament of Germany and Her Rearmament (1919-1939)*. Oxford University Press, 1946.
Rodnick, David, *Postwar Germans; An Anthropologist's Account*. Yale University Press, 1948.
Taylor, Telford, *Sword and Swastika*. Simon and Schuster, 1952.
Wheeler-Bennett, John W., *The Nemesis of Power*. Macmillan, 1953.

CHAPTER 8: AN UNDERCURRENT OF UNCERTAINTY

Connell, Brian, *A Watcher on the Rhine; An Appraisal of Germany Today*. William Morrow, 1957.
Emmet, Christopher, and Norbert Muhlen, *The Vanishing Swastika*. Henry Regnery, 1961.
Horne, Alistair, *Back into Power; A Report on the New Germany*. Max Parrish, London, 1955.
Speier, Hans, *German Rearmament and Atomic War*. Row, Peterson, 1957.

CHAPTER 9: A RESURGENCE OF INTELLECT

Bithell, Jethro, ed., *Germany; Companion to German Studies*. Pitman, 1955.
Friederich, Werner P., *An Outline-History of German Literature*. Barnes & Noble, 1961.
Haftmann, Werner, Alfred Hentzen, William S. Lieberman and Andrew Carnduff Ritchie, eds., *German Art of the Twentieth Century*. The Museum of Modern Art, 1957.
Heller, Erich, *The Disinherited Mind*. Farrar, Straus and Cudahy, 1957.
Holthusen, Hans Egon, "A Literature in Transition, Main Currents of Postwar German Writing." *Atlantic Monthly*, Vol. 199, No. 3 (March, 1957).
Kohn, Hans, *The Mind of Germany*. Charles Scribner's Sons, 1960.
Lehmann-Haupt, Hellmut, *Art Under a Dictatorship*. Oxford University Press, 1954.
Neumann, Franz L., *Behemoth; The Structure and Practice of National Socialism, 1933-1944*. Oxford University Press, 1944.
Roethel, Hans Konrad, *Modern German Painting*. Reynal, 1957.

CHAPTER 10: THE UNSETTLED AND PERILOUS FUTURE

Bathurst, M. E., and J. L. Simpson, *Germany and the North Atlantic Community*. Frederick A. Praeger, 1956.
Conant, James Bryant, *Germany and Freedom, A Personal Appraisal*. Harvard University Press, 1958.
Freund, Gerald, *Germany Between Two Worlds*. Harcourt, Brace, 1961.
McInnis, Edgar, Richard Hiscocks and Robert Spencer, *The Shaping of Postwar Germany*. Frederick A. Praeger, 1960.
Prittie, Terence, *Germany Divided, The Legacy of the Nazi Era*. Atlantic-Little, Brown, 1960.

FAMOUS GERMAN CULTURAL FIGURES AND THEIR PRINCIPAL WORKS

Music

Schütz, Heinrich	1585-1672	Church music. First German opera: *Dafne*
Telemann, Georg Philipp	1681-1767	Church music, operas, overtures, sonatas, chamber music
Handel, George Frederick	1685-1759	Oratorios: *The Messiah.* Operas, cantatas, works for harpsichord, organ, other instruments. Spent latter part of his life in Britain
Bach, Johann Sebastian	1685-1750	Church music (chorales, preludes, fugues, passion oratorios): *St. John Passion, St. Matthew Passion.* Compositions for organ and other instruments: *The Well-Tempered Clavier*
Gluck, C. W. von	1714-1787	Operas: *Orpheus and Eurydice, Iphigenia in Tauris.* Reformer of operatic style
Beethoven, Ludwig van	1770-1827	Symphonies, sonatas, chamber works. Last of great classical, first of romantic composers
Weber, Carl Maria von	1786-1826	Operas: *Der Freischütz.* Concert pieces: *Invitation to the Dance.* Masses
Mendelssohn, Felix	1809-1847	Symphonies, oratorios, songs, piano works, violin concerto. Overtures: *A Midsummer Night's Dream, The Hebrides*
Schumann, Robert	1810-1856	Symphonies, overtures, chamber music, songs. Leading romantic composer
Wagner, Richard	1813-1883	Operas: *Tannhäuser, Lohengrin, The Ring* cycle, *Tristan and Isolde, Die Meistersinger, Parsifal*
Brahms, Johannes	1833-1897	Symphonies, songs, choral works, chamber music, concertos. Outstanding romanticist
Strauss, Richard	1864-1949	Symphonic poems: *Don Juan, Death and Transfiguration, Thus Spake Zarathustra.* Operas: *Salomé, Elektra, Der Rosenkavalier.* Noted for complex modern orchestral style
Orff, Carl	1895-	Oratorios: *Carmina Burana.* Operas: *The Moon, Die Kluge.* Songs, music for the theater
Hindemith, Paul	1895-1963	Operas: *Mathis der Maler.* Sonatas, concertos, chamber music. A U.S. resident after 1939
Weill, Kurt	1900-1950	Operas: *The Threepenny Opera.* Songs, choral and orchestral works. Musicals: *Lady in the Dark*
Egk, Werner	1901-	Operas: *Irish Legend, Magic Violin, Inspector General.* Ballets, orchestral pieces

Painting, Sculpture, Architecture

Lochner, Stephan	-1451	Painter of religious subjects: the *Dombild* in Cologne Cathedral, *Virgin with the Violets*
Schongauer, Martin	c.1446-1488	Painter, engraver of historical and religious subjects: *Madonna of the Rose Arbor*
Holbein, Hans the Elder	c.1465-1524	Painter, draftsman. Historical and religious pictures: Altarpiece of St. Sebastian. Portraits
Grünewald, Mathias	c.1470-1528	Painter of religious subjects of great intensity and realism: Isenheim Altarpiece
Dürer, Albrecht	1471-1528	Painter, draftsman, engraver. Realistic portraits, religious paintings, landscapes, animal drawings: *The Knight, Melancolia, The Four Evangelists, Adoration of the Magi*
Cranach, Lucas the Elder	1472-1553	Painter, engraver: *Rest on the Flight to Egypt, Marriage of St. Catherine, Crucifixion*
Grien, Hans Baldung	c.1480-1545	Painter of religious and mythological subjects: *Coronation of the Virgin, Luxury, Death*
Huber, Wolf	1490-1553	Painter of religious subjects: *Christ's Farewell, Agony in Gethsemane, Flight into Egypt*
Holbein, Hans the Younger	1493-1543	Painter, engraver of German Renaissance period. Religious subjects: *Dead Christ, Madonna of Burgomaster Meyer.* Portraits: *Erasmus, Sir Thomas More, The Ambassadors*
Fischer, Johann Michael	1691-1766	Architect, sculptor. Leading designer of late baroque and early rococo Bavarian churches
Kollwitz, Käthe	1867-1945	Painter, lithographer, etcher. Noted for pictures of poverty, war, mothers and children
Nolde, Emil	1867-1956	Painter, illustrator. Seascapes. Garden scenes: *Sunflowers.* Supernatural and religious subjects: *The Last Supper, Masks, Death of Mary of Egypt.* A founder of Expressionist school
Barlach, Ernst	1870-1938	Sculptor, writer. Wood and bronze sculptures, lithographs
Kolbe, Georg	1877-1947	Sculptor. Figure studies, bronzes, public monuments in Berlin, Hamburg, Leipzig
Marc, Franz	1880-1916	Expressionist painter of landscapes, animals: *Red Horse.* A leader of Blaue Reiter abstractionists
Kirchner, Ernst Ludwig	1880-1938	Painter, designer: *Street Scene, Rhine Bridge.* Pioneer of Expressionist school
Lehmbruck, Wilhelm	1881-1919	Expressionist sculptor: *Kneeling Woman*
Gropius, Walter	1883-	Architect. Leader of functional school, founder of the Bauhaus. Emigrated to U.S. in 1937
Heckel, Erich	1883-	Expressionist painter: *A Crystal Day, Two Men at a Table, White Horses*
Beckmann, Max	1884-1950	Painter, engraver in Expressionist style: *The Bridge, Woman Reclining, Departure*
Schmidt-Rottluff, Karl	1884-	Expressionist painter, sculptor, engraver. Noted for etchings, mosaics, tapestries, oils
Mies van der Rohe, Ludwig	1886-	Architect. A Bauhaus founder who has worked in the U.S. since the 1930s: buildings for Illinois Institute of Technology; apartment houses; Seagram Building, New York
Macke, August	1887-1914	Expressionist painter: *Portrait of Franz Marc, Four Women, Boulevard, Mobilization*
Mendelsohn, Erich	1887-1953	Expressionist architect: Albert Einstein Tower, Potsdam; Maimonides Hospital, San Francisco
Marcks, Gerhard	1889-	Sculptor, mainly in classical tradition. Worked with Gropius at the Bauhaus
Ernst, Max	1891-	Painter, writer: *Monument to Birds, The Eye of Silence.* Leader of surrealists and earlier dadaists

Literature (Austrian writers are included on the following list)

Hartmann von Aue	c.1170-c.1215	Epics: *Erec, Iwein.* Religious legends: *Gregorius, Der arme Heinrich*
Wolfram von Eschenbach	c.1170-c.1220	Epics: *Parzival, Willehalm*
Luther, Martin	1483-1546	German translation of the Bible. Pamphlets. Religious songs
Kant, Immanuel	1724-1804	Philosophy: *Critique of Pure Reason, Critique of Practical Reason*
Klopstock, Friedrich Gottlieb	1724-1803	Epic: *Der Messias.* Odes
Lessing, Gotthold Ephraim	1729-1781	Plays: *Minna von Barnhelm, Nathan the Wise.* Critical and philosophical essays
Herder, Johann Gottfried	1744-1803	Essays. Collections of folk songs
Goethe, Johann Wolfgang von	1749-1832	Plays: *Faust, Iphigenia in Tauris.* Novels: *The Sorrows of Young Werther.* Poems. Essays
Schiller, Johann Friedrich von	1759-1805	Plays: *Mary Stuart, William Tell, The Maid of Orleans, Don Carlos.* Poems
Schlegel, August Wilhelm von	1767-1845	Theorist of romanticism. Translations of Shakespeare, Dante, Cervantes. Literary criticism

Schlegel, Friedrich von	1772-1829	Theorist of romanticism. Experimental works: *Lucinde, Alarcos.* Philosophy
Schleiermacher, Friedrich	1768-1834	Philosophy: *The Christian Faith*
Hegel, Georg Wilhelm Friedrich	1770-1831	Philosophy: *Phenomenology of Mind, Philosophy of Right*
Hölderlin, Friedrich	1770-1843	Novel: *Hyperion.* Poems
Novalis (von Hardenberg)	1772-1801	Novel: *Heinrich von Ofterdingen.* Poems: *Hymnen an die Nacht*
Schelling, F. W. von	1775-1854	Philosophy: *Ideen zu einer Philosophie der Natur*
Hoffmann, E.T.A.	1776-1822	Tales: *Weird Tales, The Nutcracker and the Mouse-King*
Kleist, Heinrich von	1777-1811	Plays: *Penthesilea, Der Prinz von Homburg.* Stories. Novels
Brentano, Clemens	1778-1842	Folk song collection: *Des Knaben Wunderhorn* (with Ludwig Achim von Arnim)
Grimm, Jakob Ludwig	1785-1863	Philology. Mythology. Folklore collection: *Fairy Tales* (with brother Wilhelm Karl Grimm)
Eichendorff, Josef von	1788-1857	Romantic poems: *Happy Wanderer and Other Poems.* Tales
Grillparzer, Franz	1791-1872	Plays: *Des Meeres und der Liebe Wellen, Der Traum: ein Leben.* Novella: *The Poor Minstrel*
Ranke, Leopold von	1795-1886	Many volumes on world history
Heine, Heinrich	1797-1856	Poems: *Last Poems, Poems, Prose and Poetry.* Travel sketches. Satires. Political writings
Büchner, Georg	1813-1837	Plays: *Danton's Death, Leonce and Lena, Wozzeck*
Hebbel, Christian Friedrich	1813-1863	Plays: *Judith, Maria Magdalena, Herod and Mariamne, The Nibelungs.* Poems. Diaries
Mommsen, Theodor	1817-1903	History: *History of Rome*
Marx, Karl	1818-1883	Philosophy: *Das Kapital, Communist Manifesto* (with Friedrich Engels). Historical writings
Fontane, Theodor	1819-1898	Novels: *L'Adultera, Trials and Tribulations, Effi Briest.* Poems
Nietzsche, Friedrich	1844-1900	Philosophy: *Thus Spake Zarathustra, The Birth of Tragedy, Beyond Good and Evil.* Poems
Freud, Sigmund	1856-1939	Founder of psychoanalysis: *The Interpretation of Dreams*
Hauptmann, Gerhart	1862-1946	Plays: *Before Dawn, The Weavers, The Sunken Bell, Rose Bernd.* Novels
Schnitzler, Arthur	1862-1931	Plays: *Anatol, Light-O'-Love, La Ronde, Professor Bernhardi.* Novels
Weber, Max	1864-1920	Sociological works: *Protestant Ethic and the Spirit of Capitalism, General Economic History*
George, Stefan	1868-1933	Poems: *Der Siebente Ring, Das Jahr der Seele, Der Teppich des Lebens*
Hofmannsthal, Hugo von	1874-1929	Librettos: *Der Rosenkavalier, Ariadne at Naxos.* Poems
Mann, Thomas	1875-1955	Novels: *The Magic Mountain, Buddenbrooks, Joseph and His Brothers, Doctor Faustus.* Stories
Rilke, Rainer Maria	1875-1926	Poems: *Duino Elegies, Sonnets to Orpheus, Requiem, Poems, Selected Poems, Later Poems*
Hesse, Hermann	1877-1962	Novels: *Demian, Steppenwolf, Magister Ludi.* Stories
Kafka, Franz	1883-1924	Novels: *The Trial, The Castle, Amerika.* Stories: *Metamorphosis, The Penal Colony*
Heidegger, Martin	1889-	Philosophy: *Existence and Being, Vom Wesen des Grundes, Was ist Metaphysik?*
Brecht, Bertolt	1898-1956	Plays: *Threepenny Opera, Mother Courage, Good Woman of Setzuan.* Poems
Grass, Günter	1927-	Novels: *The Tin Drum, Cat and Mouse, Dog Years*

Science

Kepler, Johannes	1571-1630	Astronomer, mathematician. Propounded laws of planetary motion
Guericke, Otto von	1602-1686	Physicist. Invented the air pump, air balance
Leibniz, G. W. von	1646-1716	Philosopher, mathematician. Developed differential and integral calculus
Humboldt, Alexander von	1769-1859	Scientist, explorer, natural philosopher
Gauss, Karl Friedrich	1777-1855	Mathematician, astronomer. Wrote on theory of numbers, binomial equations
Wohler, Friedrich	1800-1882	Chemist. Discovered aluminum. Conducted experiments leading to first synthesis of an organic compound
Liebig, Justus von	1803-1873	Chemist. Improved organic analysis. Contributed valuably to agricultural chemistry
Bunsen, Robert	1811-1899	Chemist. Discovered method of spectrum analysis (with Kirchhoff), rubidium, cesium
Helmholtz, H. L. von	1821-1894	Physiologist, physicist. Noted for discoveries in optics and acoustics
Virchow, Rudolf	1821-1902	Pathologist. A founder of cellular pathology
Clausius, R. J. E.	1822-1888	Physicist. Formulated second law of thermodynamics
Kirchhoff, Gustav Robert	1824-1887	Physicist. Discovered method of spectrum analysis (with Bunsen). Founded astrophysics
Riemann, G. F. B.	1826-1866	Mathematician. Worked on complex variables, method of representing them, non-Euclidian geometry
Koch, Robert	1843-1910	Bacteriologist. Discovered bacterial cause of many infectious diseases: anthrax, tuberculosis
Pfeffer, Wilhelm	1845-1920	Plant physiologist. Synthesized fundamentals of plant physiology
Röntgen, Wilhelm Konrad	1845-1923	Physicist. Discovered X rays
Fischer, Emil	1852-1919	Chemist. Pioneered in organic chemistry, discovered structures of sugars, proteins, purines
Ostwald, Wilhelm	1853-1932	Physical chemist, philosopher. Investigated principles governing equilibrium, reaction rates
Ehrlich, Paul	1854-1915	Biochemist. Discovered salvarsan arsenicals. Developed lateral chain theory of immunization
Hertz, Heinrich Rudolf	1857-1894	Physicist. Investigated relation between electricity, light. Discovered waves used in telegraphy
Planck, Max	1858-1947	Physicist. Formulated quantum theory
Nernst, Walther Hermann	1864-1941	Physicist, chemist. Formulated third law of thermodynamics. A founder of modern physical chemistry
Hahn, Otto	1879-1968	Physical chemist. Discovered several radioactive substances. Formed artificial radioactive elements. Split uranium atom (1939), showed possibility of chain reactions
Einstein, Albert	1879-1955	Theoretical physicist. Explained the photoelectric effect. Developed special and general theories of relativity. Emigrated to U.S. in 1933
Laue, Max von	1879-1960	Physicist. Discovered diffraction of X rays by a crystal. Specialized in theoretical physics
Staudinger, Hermann	1881-1965	Chemist. Studied macro-molecule, leading to expansion of plastics, artificial fiber industries
Heisenberg, Werner	1901-	Physicist. Developed theory of quantum mechanics. Discovered allotropic forms of hydrogen

Credits

The sources for the illustrations in this book appear below. Credits for pictures from left to right are separated by commas, from top to bottom by dashes.

Cover—Robert E. Lackenbach from Black Star
8, 9—Marvin E. Newman
12—Chart by John Woods
17, 18, 19—Ralph Crane
20, 21—Ralph Crane except bottom right Sabine Weiss from Rapho Guillumette
22, 23—James Whitmore
24, 25—Dmitri Kessel
26, 27—Robert E. Lackenbach from Black Star, Eliot Elisofon
28—Mark Kauffman
29—Robert E. Lackenbach from Black Star
30, 31—Ralph Crane
32, 33—The Bettmann Archive
39—Maps by Matt Greene
42, 43—Brown Brothers—M. T. Bonney, European Picture Service
44—European Picture Service—Culver Pictures
45 through 51—Hugo Jaeger
52—STERN from Black Star
60, 61—Margaret Bourke-White, Ralph Crane
62, 63—Walter Sanders
64—Henri Cartier-Bresson from Magnum
65—Scheler-STERN from Black Star—Ralph Crane
66, 67—Left: Sven Simon—Walter Sanders; center: J. H. Darchinger, Bonn—Loomis Dean; right: D. P. A. Pictorial
68—Erich Hartmann from Magnum for FORTUNE
72—Map by John Woods
75—Ralph Crane
76—Stan Wayman
77—Erich Lessing from Magnum
78, 79—Pierre Boulat for TIME
80, 81—Ralph Crane except right Pierre Boulat for TIME
82—Pierre Boulat for TIME
83—Ralph Crane
84—John Launois from Black Star
85—James Whitmore
86, 87—Walter Sanders
88, 89—Burk Uzzle
94, 95—Erich Lessing from Magnum, Ralph Crane
96, 97—Hannes Betzler, D.P.A.-Pictorial
98, 99—Left: Ralph Crane; center: Erich Lessing from Magnum; right: Robert E. Lackenbach from Black Star
100—Erich Lessing from Magnum
101, 102, 103—Jochen Blume
104—Ralph Crane
106—Map by Matt Greene
111—Robert E. Lackenbach from Black Star
112—Wide World Photos
114, 115—Left: Ralph Crane—James Whitmore; right: Henri Cartier-Bresson from Magnum
116, 117—Walter Sanders
118—*Simplicissimus,* Munich
122, 123—Henri Cartier-Bresson from Magnum except right Hannes Betzler
124, 125—Hannes Betzler, Hannes Betzler from Black Star
126, 127—Left: D.P.A.-Pictorial; right: Don Uhrbrock
128, 129—Robert E. Lackenbach from Black Star
135, 136—Ralph Crane
137—Michael Rougier
138, 139—Robert E. Lackenbach from Black Star, Dennis Stock from Magnum
140—Tom Hollyman from Photo Researchers, Inc.
145—Drawing by Jerome Snyder
149—Courtesy Ehemals Staatliche Museen Berlin Dahlem
150—Courtesy Alte Pinakothek Munich
151—Dmitri Kessel courtesy Alte Pinakothek Munich
152, 153—Eric Schaal courtesy Museum of Colmar France
154—Courtesy Ehemals Staatliche Museen Berlin Dahlem
156—Courtesy Museum of Modern Art, New York
157—Courtesy Morton D. May
158—Courtesy Museum of Modern Art, New York, gift of Dr. W. R. Valentiner—courtesy Kurt Deschler Collection
159—Ken Schmid courtesy collection Staatliche Kunstsammlungen, Stuttgart
160—Dan Weiner for SPORTS ILLUSTRATED
165—Pierre Boulat
166, 167—Michael Friedel

ACKNOWLEDGMENTS

The editors of this book received valuable assistance from the following scholars: Leonard Krieger, Professor of History, University of Chicago; Richard Plant, Associate Professor of German, City College of New York; Joseph Rothschild, Professor of Government, Columbia University; and Mark Kesselman, Assistant Professor of Government, Columbia University.

Index

**This symbol in front of a page number indicates a photograph or painting of the subject mentioned.*

xxxx

Production staff for Time Incorporated

John L. Hallenbeck (Vice President and Director of Production)

Robert E. Foy and Caroline Ferri

Text photocomposed under the direction of

Albert J. Dunn and Arthur J. Dunn

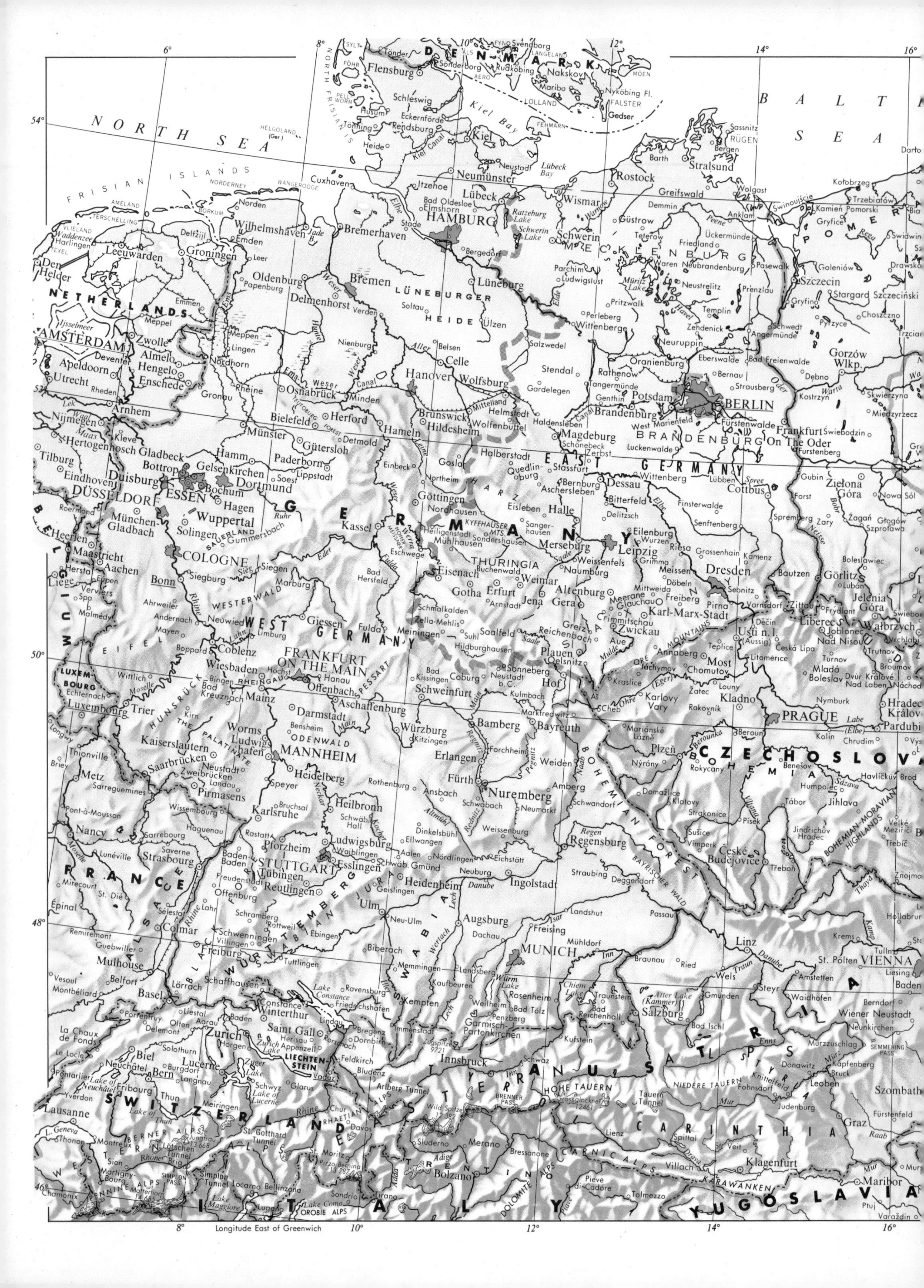
6°
8°
10°
12°
14°
16°
54°
52°
50°
48°
46°
NORTH SEA
BALTIC SEA
FRISIAN ISLANDS
NORTH FRISIAN IS.
HELGOLAND (Ger.)
NORDERNEY
WANGEROOGE
AMELAND
TERSCHELLING
VLIELAND
TEXEL
BORKUM
SYLT
FÖHR
PELLWORM
FYN
LANGELAND
AERO
LOLLAND
FALSTER
MÖEN
FEHMARN
RÜGEN
DENMARK
Tönder
Svendborg
Sonderborg
Rudköbing
Nakskov
Maribo
Nykøbing Fl.
Gedser
Flensburg
Schleswig
Husum
Eckernförde
Tönning
Rendsburg
Heide
Kiel
Kiel Bay
Kiel Canal
Neustadt
Lübeck Bay
Neumünster
Itzehoe
Cuxhaven
Bad Oldesloe
Elmshorn
Lübeck
Stade
HAMBURG
Ratzeburg Lake
Schwerin Lake
Bergedorf
Wismar
Schwerin
Rostock
Barth
Stralsund
Bergen
Sassnitz
Greifswald
Wolgast
Demmin
Anklam
Güstrow
Teterow
Friedland
Ückermünde
MECKLENBURG
Parchim
Ludwigslust
Waren
Neubrandenburg
Müritz Lake
Neustrelitz
Pasewalk
Prenzlau
Templin
Zehdenick
Schwedt
Angermünde
Eberswalde
Bad Freienwalde
Pritzwalk
Perleberg
Wittenberge
Neuruppin
Oranienburg
Bernau
Strausberg
Rathenow
Tangermünde
Genthin
Potsdam
BERLIN
Brandenburg
West Marienfeld
Fürstenwalde
Frankfurt On The Oder
Fürstenberg
BRANDENBURG
Luckenwalde
Salzwedel
Stendal
Gardelegen
Lüneburg
LÜNEBURGER HEIDE
Soltau
Ülzen
Celle
Belsen
Wolfsburg
Mittelland Canal
Helmstedt
Haldensleben
Magdeburg
Schönebeck
Zerbst
Halberstadt
Quedlinburg
Stassfurt
EAST GERMANY
Wittenberg
Dessau
Bernburg
Aschersleben
Köthen
Lübben
Spree
Cottbus
Bitterfeld
Finsterwalde
Senftenberg
Eisleben
Halle
Delitzsch
Sangerhausen
Merseburg
Leipzig
Eilenburg
Wurzen
Riesa
Grossenhain
Kamenz
Weissenfels
Naumburg
Grimma
Meissen
Dresden
Döbeln
Bautzen
Görlitz
Mittweida
Freiberg
Pirna
Sebnitz
Zittau
Varnsdorf
Altenburg
Meerane
Glauchau
Karl-Marx-Stadt
Crimmitschau
Zwickau
Gera
Jena
Weimar
Erfurt
Gotha
Arnstadt
Eisenach
THURINGIA
Buchenwald
Mühlhausen
Sondershausen
Heiligenstadt
KYFFHÄUSER MTS.
HARZ
Nordhausen
Göttingen
Northeim
Goslar
Einbeck
Hildesheim
Wolfenbüttel
Brunswick
Hanover
Hameln
Minden
Herford
Bielefeld
Detmold
TEUTOBURG FOREST
Gütersloh
Paderborn
Lippstadt
Soest
Münster
Hamm
Osnabrück
Rheine
Nordhorn
Lingen
Meppen
Emden
Leer
Papenburg
Oldenburg
Delmenhorst
Bremen
Verden
Nienburg
Bremerhaven
Wilhelmshaven
Jade B.
Norden
Emmen
Gronau
Bocholt
Gladbeck
Bottrop
Gelsenkirchen
Dortmund
Bochum
ESSEN
Duisburg
DÜSSELDORF
Hagen
Wuppertal
Ruhr
Solingen
SAUERLAND
Gummersbach
Mönchen-Gladbach
COLOGNE
Siegen
Siegburg
Bonn
Aachen
Eupen
Verviers
Spa
Malmédy
Ahrweiler
Andernach
Neuwied
Mayen
EIFEL
WESTERWALD
Coblenz
Boppard
Limburg
Lahn
Giessen
Marburg
Wiesbaden
Höchst
FRANKFURT ON THE MAIN
Hanau
Offenbach
Mainz
Bingen
RHEINGAU
Bad Kreuznach
HUNSRÜCK
Trier
Wittlich
Echternach
LUXEMBOURG
Luxembourg
Kirn
THE PALATINATE
Worms
Ludwigshafen
Kaiserslautern
Saarbrücken
Neustadt
Zweibrücken
Pirmasens
Landau
Wissembourg
Haguenau
MANNHEIM
Heidelberg
Darmstadt
Bensheim
ODENWALD
Aschaffenburg
SPESSART
Fulda
Bad Hersfeld
Kassel
Eschwege
Werra
Eder
Meiningen
Schmalkalden
Zella-Mehlis
Suhl
Hildburghausen
Saalfeld
Sonneberg
Coburg
Neustadt b.C.
Kulmbach
Hof
Plauen
Oelsnitz
Reichenbach
Greiz
Aue
Annaberg
ORE MOUNTAINS
Bad Kissingen
Schweinfurt
Würzburg
Kitzingen
Bamberg
Bayreuth
Marktredwitz
Erlangen
Forchheim
Fürth
Nuremberg
Schwabach
Neumarkt
Amberg
Weiden
Schwandorf
Regensburg
Rothenburg
Ansbach
Dinkelsbühl
Ellwangen
Aalen
Nördlingen
Eichstätt
Heilbronn
Schwäb. Hall
Bruchsal
Karlsruhe
Rastatt
Pforzheim
Ludwigsburg
Waiblingen
Esslingen
STUTTGART
Schwäb. Gmünd
Tübingen
Reutlingen
Baden-Baden
Freudenstadt
Offenburg
Geislingen
Heidenheim
Ulm
Neu-Ulm
Ingolstadt
Neuburg
Danube
Straubing
Deggendorf
Passau
Landshut
Augsburg
Dachau
Freising
Mühldorf
MUNICH
Biberach
Memmingen
Landsberg
Kaufbeuren
Kempten
Weilheim
Bad Tölz
Rosenheim
Traunstein
Bad Reichenhall
Penzberg
Garmisch-Partenkirchen
Zugspitze 9721
Ravensburg
Friedrichshafen
Lake Constance
Lindau
Bregenz
Dornbirn
Schramberg
Rottweil
Schwenningen
Villingen
Ebingen
Tuttlingen
Freiburg
Lörrach
Schaffhausen
WÜRTTEMBERG
SWABIAN JURA
SWABIA
BLACK FOREST
WEST GERMANY
GERMANY
Lahr
Sélestat
Colmar
Strasbourg
Saverne
Sarrebourg
Lunéville
Nancy
Pont-à-Mousson
Metz
Sarreguemines
Thionville
Longwy
Briey
ALSACE
FRANCE
Mirecourt
St. Dié
Épinal
Remiremont
Guebwiller
Mulhouse
Belfort
Vesoul
Montbéliard
Basel
Porrentruy
Delemont
Liestal
Olten
Aarau
Baden
Winterthur
Zurich
Horgen
Zurich Lake
Saint Gall
Herisau
Appenzell
Rorschach
Konstanz
Solothurn
Biel
Lucerne
Zuger Lake
Schwyz
Lake of Lucerne
LIECHTENSTEIN
Vaduz
Feldkirch
Bludenz
Glarus
Chur
Davos
Neuchâtel
Lake of Neuchâtel
Bern
Burgdorf
Langnau
Thun
Lake of Thun
La Chaux de Fonds
Le Locle
Pontarlier
Yverdon
Fribourg
Lausanne
L. Geneva
Thonon
Montreux
Meiringen
SWITZERLAND
BERNER ALPS
Jungfrau 13,668
Lötschen Tunnel
St. Gotthard Tunnel
Brig
Sion
Martigny-Bourg
Simplon Tunnel
SIMPLON PASS
PENNINE ALPS
Matterhorn 14,685
Chamonix
Locarno
Bellinzona
Lake Maggiore
Lugano
Lake Como
OROBIE ALPS
Sondrio
Tirano
St. Moritz
Pizzo Bernina 13,287
RHAETIAN ALPS
Rhine
Arlberg Tunnel
Innsbruck
Schwaz
Kufstein
BRENNER PASS
Wild Spitze 12,382
Sluderno
Merano
Bressanone
Bolzano
Adige
TRENTINO ALPS
DOLOMITE ALPS
Pieve di Cadore
Tolmezzo
CARNIC ALPS
HOHE TAUERN
Grossglockner 12,461
Lienz
Tauern Tunnel
Spittal
St. Veit
Villach
Klagenfurt
KARAWANKEN
CARINTHIA
Drava
EASTERN ALPS
TYROL
AUSTRIA
Salzburg
Chiem Lake
Atter Lake (Kammer)
Gmunden
Bad Ischl
Steyr
Wels
Traun
Linz
Braunau
Ried
Danube
Enns
NIEDERE TAUERN
Fohnsdorf
Judenburg
Knittelfeld
Leoben
Bruck
Kapfenberg
Donawitz
Mürzzuschlag
SEMMERING PASS
STYRIA
Graz
Raab
Fürstenfeld
Maribor
Mur
Ptuj
Varaždin
YUGOSLAVIA
Amstetten
Waidhofen
St. Pölten
VIENNA
Krems
Tulln
Liesing
Baden
Berndorf
Wiener Neustadt
Neunkirchen
Szombathely
Hollabrunn
Znojmo
Thaya
Kamp
ITALY
Dečín
Ústí n.L. (Aussig)
Teplice
Most
Chomutov
Jáchymov
Karlovy Vary
Cheb
Kraslice
Ohre (Eger)
Žatec
Louny
Kladno
Rakovník
Mariánské Lázně
Plzeň
Berounka
Beroun
PRAGUE
Labe (Elbe)
Kolín
Nymburk
Chrudim
Pardubice
Hradec Králové
Mladá Boleslav
Turnov
Dvůr Králové nad Labem
Náchod
Česká Lípa
Liberec
Jablonec nad Nisou
Trutnov
Broumov
Vrchlabí
CZECHOSLOVAKIA
BOHEMIA
Rokycany
Nýřany
Domažlice
Klatovy
Strakonice
Písek
Sušice
Vimperk
České Budějovice
Třeboň
Tábor
Jindřichův Hradec
Benešov
Humpolec
Jihlava
Havlíčkův Brod
Sázava
Vltava
Velké Meziříčí
Třebíč
BOHEMIAN-MORAVIAN HIGHLANDS
BOHEMIAN FOREST
BAYRISCHER WALD
Szczecin
Swinoujście
Kamień Pomorski
Gryfice
Trzebiatów
Kołobrzeg
Goleniów
Stargard Szczeciński
Gryfino
Pyrzyce
Choszczno
POMERANIA
Gorzów Wlkp.
Dębno
Kostrzyn
Skwierzyna
Międzyrzecz
Świebodzin
Gubin
Zielona Góra
Nowa Sól
Forst
Żagań
Żary
Szprotawa
Głogów
Bolesławiec
Lubań
Jelenia Góra
Wałbrzych
Frýdlant
Warta
Oder
Neisse
Drawsko
Świdwin
Spremberg
Longitude East of Greenwich